The Wiersbe
BIBLE STUDY SERIES

The
Wiersbe
BIBLE STUDY SERIES

Determining

to Go God's

Direction

DANIEL

David C Cook®
transforming lives together

THE WIERSBE BIBLE STUDY SERIES: DANIEL
Published by David C. Cook
4050 Lee Vance View
Colorado Springs, CO 80918 U.S.A.

David C. Cook Distribution Canada
55 Woodslee Avenue, Paris, Ontario, Canada N3L 3E5

David C. Cook U.K., Kingsway Communications
Eastbourne, East Sussex BN23 6NT, England

All excerpts taken from *Be Resolute,* second edition, published by
David C. Cook in 2008 © 2000 Warren W. Wiersbe, ISBN 978-1-4347-6781-3

ISBN 978-0-7814-4569-6

The Team: Steve Parolini, Karen Lee-Thorp,
Amy Kiechlin, Jack Campbell, and Susan Vannaman
Series Cover Design: John Hamilton Design
Cover Photo: Veer Inc., Photodisc Photography

Printed in the United States of America
First Edition 2009

2 3 4 5 6 7 8 9 10

032008

Contents

Introduction to Daniel

The Prophet Daniel

What Jesus said about the prophet John the Baptist we could say about the prophet Daniel: "What did you go out into the wilderness to see? A reed shaken by the wind? ... But what did you go out to see? A prophet? Yes, I say to you, and more than a prophet" (Matt. 11:7, 9 NKJV).

Daniel dared to be different. Instead of bending and blending like a reed, he stood like a mighty oak, rooted in the Lord and defying the storms of change that raged about him.

The Sovereign Lord

Today's society is a good deal like the one Daniel lived in centuries ago. The world still wants God's people to conform to its standards and follow its practices. "Don't let the world around you squeeze you into its own mold" is the way J. B. Phillips translates Romans 12:2, and Daniel and his friends obeyed that admonition.

As we study the book of Daniel, we'll meet Daniel's God, the Sovereign Lord who rules in the kingdom of men (Dan. 4:32) and who confidently announces things to come. In Daniel's life and ministry we see how true believers live in the light of biblical prophecy—how they relate to the Sovereign Lord and accomplish His good, acceptable, and perfect will.

—*Warren W. Wiersbe*

How to Use This Study

This study is designed for both individual and small-group use. We've divided it into ten lessons—each references one or more chapters in Warren W. Wiersbe's commentary *Be Resolute* (second edition, David C. Cook, 2008). While reading *Be Resolute* is not a prerequisite for going through this study, the additional insights and background Wiersbe offers can greatly enhance your study experience.

The **Getting Started** questions at the beginning of each lesson offer you an opportunity to record your first thoughts and reactions to the study text. This is an important step in the study process as those "first impressions" often include clues about what it is your heart is longing to discover.

The bulk of the study is found in the **Going Deeper** questions. These dive into the Bible text and, along with helpful excerpts from Wiersbe's commentary, help you examine not only the original context and meaning of the verses but also modern application.

Looking Inward narrows the focus down to your personal story. These intimate questions can be a bit uncomfortable at times, but don't shy away from honesty here. This is where you are asked to stand before the mirror of God's Word and look closely at what you see. It's the place to take a good look at yourself in light of the lesson and search for ways in which you can grow in faith.

Going Forward is the place where you can commit to paper those things you want or need to do in order to better live out the discoveries you made in the Looking Inward section. Don't skip or skim through this. Take the time to really consider what practical steps you might take to move closer to Christ. Then share your thoughts with a trusted friend who can act as an encourager and accountability partner.

Finally, there is a brief **Seeking Help** section to close the lesson. This is a reminder for you to invite God into your spiritual-growth process. If you choose to write out a prayer in this section, come back to it as you work through the lesson and continue to seek the Holy Spirit's guidance as you discover God's will for your life.

Tips for Small Groups

A small group is a dynamic thing. One week it might seem like a group of close-knit friends. The next it might seem more like a group of uncomfortable strangers. A small-group leader's role is to read these subtle changes and adjust the tone of the discussion accordingly.

Small groups need to be safe places for people to talk openly. It is through shared wrestling with difficult life issues that some of the greatest personal growth is discovered. But in order for the group to feel safe, participants need to know it's okay *not* to share sometimes. Always invite honest disclosure, but never force someone to speak if he or she isn't comfortable doing so. (A savvy leader will follow up later with a group member who isn't comfortable sharing in a group setting to see if a one-on-one discussion is more appropriate.)

Have volunteers take turns reading excerpts from Scripture or from the commentary. The more each person is involved even in the mundane tasks, the more he or she will feel comfortable opening up in more meaningful ways.

Finally, soak your group meetings in prayer—before you begin, during as needed, and always at the end of your time together.

God Rules

(DANIEL I)

Before you begin …

- *Pray for the Holy Spirit to reveal truth and wisdom as you go through this lesson.*
- *Read Daniel 1. This lesson references chapter 1 in* Be Resolute. *It will be helpful for you to have your Bible and a copy of the commentary available as you work through this lesson.*

Getting Started

From the Commentary

Though not a professed evangelical believer, [Benjamin] Franklin was a man who believed in a God who is the Architect and Governor of the universe, a conviction that agrees with the testimony of Scripture. Abraham called God "the Judge of all the earth" (Gen. 18:25), and King Hezekiah prayed, "Thou art the God, even thou alone, of all the kingdoms of the earth" (2 Kings 19:15). In Daniel's day, King Nebuchadnezzar learned the hard way that "the Most High is sovereign over the kingdoms of men" (Dan. 4:32 NIV).

The first chapter of Daniel's book gives ample evidence of the sovereign hand of God in the affairs of both nations and individuals.

—*Be Resolute,* pages 17–18

1. *A:* Circle phrases or words in Daniel 1 that point to the sovereignty of God. *B* How does this opening story set the table for the rest of the book? *C* Why was the sovereignty of God such an important topic to the Israelites? *D:* Why might they have had reason to question God's sovereignty?

A: 1:2 1:9 1:17, 1:20, 1:21 1:15

B: God is in control. Daniel was a model.

C: Their history and future depends on their relationship with a God - their God in control.

D: They have been exiled to Babylon. Captivity

Babylonian culture was secular, rich and mighty

More to Consider: Note in Daniel 1:20 the almost casual reference to "magicians and enchanters." Why do you think the king grouped Daniel and his friends with these folks? What does this say about the Babylonian culture? He thought they could foretell natural eve Magicians invoke the supernatural using charms, spells or rituals.

2. Choose one verse or phrase from Daniel 1 that stands out to you. This could be something you're intrigued by, something that makes you

uncomfortable, something that puzzles you, something that resonates with you, or just something you want to examine further. Write that here. What strikes you about this verse?

1:8 - Daniel resolved he would not defile hemself with the King's food and drink.

Going Deeper

From the Commentary

> For decades, the prophets had warned the rulers of Judah that their idolatry, immorality, and injustice toward the poor and needy would lead to the nation's ruin. The prophets saw the day coming when God would bring the Babylonian army to destroy Jerusalem and the temple and take the people captive to Babylon.
>
> —*Be Resolute*, page 18

3. Review Isaiah 13:1–4, 39:1–8, and Micah 4:10. What prophesies do these passages give about the Babylonian captivity? In what ways are these passages another example of God's sovereignty?

Concerns Babylon's doom - He set the armies apart. They are his weapons and carry his anger. God will rescue Israel from the grip of their enemies - (God brought back the faithful)

From the Commentary

> So wise and powerful is our God that He can permit
> men and women to make personal choices and still
> accomplish His purposes in this world. When He isn't
> permitted to rule, He will overrule, but His will shall
> ultimately be done and His name glorified. We worship
> and serve a sovereign God who is never caught by sur-
> prise. No matter what our circumstances may be, we can
> always say with confidence, "Alleluia! … The Lord God
> Omnipotent reigns!" (Rev. 19:6 NKJV).
>
> —*Be Resolute*, page 19

4. What surprises you about Daniel's response to the Babylonian official
in 1:8 and 1:12–14? How does God use Daniel's polite defiance to glorify
Himself? What are other examples that show how God uses our personal
choices to further His kingdom?

He asked the official's permission not to defile himself with the rich food and drink -

after their 10 day period of vegetables and water, they were better in appearance than others eating the King's rich food.

Caring for others - Katrina Disaster

From the History Books

The city of Babylon was built along the Euphrates River (in what is now
Iraq), with portions of the city on either side of the river. Between 1770 and

1670 BC, and again between 612 and 320 BC, it may have been the largest city in the world (reaching a population of more than 200,000). One archaeological study estimates that the square wall around the city measured 42 miles in length, while another estimates it was as many as 56 miles long. The walls were purportedly 24 meters wide. However, as impressive as the city was, it was also beset with political strife and besieged more than once by neighboring nations, including the Assyrians and the Persians (as noted in the book of Daniel).

5. *A.* How does the immensity and importance of Babylon play into Daniel's story? *B.* What does it say about God's intent for the Israelites during this chapter of their long story? *C.* How much more significant is Daniel's denial to obey the king's decree in light of what you read about Babylon's history?

A - It was a rich and powerful and secular City.

B - God's intent was to rescue them.

C - He was not threaten by the history.

From the Commentary

Even a cursory reading of the Old Testament reveals that the majority of God's people have not always followed the Lord and kept His commandments. It has always been the "faithful remnant" within the Jewish nation that has come through the trials and judgments to maintain the divine covenant and make a new beginning. The prophet Isaiah named one of his sons "Shear-jashub," which means "a remnant shall return" (Isa. 7:3). The same principle applies to the church today, for not everybody who professes faith in Jesus Christ is truly a child of God (Matt. 7:21–23). In His messages to the seven churches of Asia Minor, our Lord always had a special word for "the overcomers," the faithful remnant in each congregation who sought to obey the Lord (Rev. 2:7, 11, 17, 24–28; 3:4–5, 12, 21). Daniel and his three friends were a part of the faithful Jewish remnant in Babylon, placed there by the Lord to accomplish His purposes.

—*Be Resolute*, pages 19–20

6. How can you tell that Daniel and his friends were part of the "faithful remnant" Wiersbe refers to in the previous excerpt? What role does confidence in God play in those who are faithful? How is this played out in Daniel's story? In stories of other faithful followers?

They followed God's will - obeyed God.
Daniel trusted God and had self assurance.

Esther and Ruth

More to Consider: The name Daniel means "God is my judge," but it was changed to Belteshazzar or "Bel protect his life." Hananiah means "the Lord shows grace," but Shadrach means "command of Aku [the moon-god]." Mishael means "Who is like God?" while Meshach means "Who is as Aku is?" Azariah means "the Lord is my help," but Abednego means "servant of Nebo." Why did the Babylonians change these men's names? What did they think it would accomplish? Knowing how important names were to the Jewish people, how might these young men have responded to being given new names?

Babyloneans wanted them to become like them – New identity – They could have rebeled

From the Commentary

How can God's people resist the pressures that can "squeeze" them into conformity with the world? According to Romans 12:1–2, "conformers" are people whose lives are controlled by pressure from without, but "transformers" are people whose lives are controlled by power from within. Daniel and his three friends were transformers: Instead of being changed, they did the changing! God used them to transform the minds of powerful rulers and to bring great glory to His name in a pagan land.

—*Be Resolute*, page 22

Romans 13:1–7

In their situation, it does not mesh with Romans 13:1–7

7. Review Romans 12:1–2. Though Daniel 1 tells about four friends who choose not to conform, other Israelites may have conformed to the king's decree. How did Daniel decide this was an appropriate time to choose not to conform? How does this mesh with the command in Romans 13:1–7 to submit to authorities?

To conform would have been against God's will – By not conforming, the King realized Daniel's God was the true God.

From the Commentary

> If you want to make a living, you get training; and if you
> want to make a life, you add education. But if you want
> to have a ministry for God, you must have divine gifts and
> divine help. Training and education are very important,
> but they are not substitutes for the ability and wisdom that
> only God can give.
>
> —*Be Resolute*, page 24

8. What does divine help look like in Daniel's story? If God works according to His own plan, that means He doesn't always "show up" when we
expect. How did Daniel overcome the fear of God letting him down? How
do Christians today overcome this fear? How does this fear incapacitate
Christians' ability to do God's will?

God is showing up in Daniel's story -
God gave Daniel understanding and wisdom -
in all his visions and dreams -
Today - Christians have to pray and ask
God for answers -

From the Commentary

> During Daniel's long life, he had opportunity to witness
> to Nebuchadnezzar, Darius, Belshazzar, and Cyrus, as well
> as to the many court officers who came and went. He was

a faithful servant, and he could say with the Lord Jesus, "I have glorified You on the earth. I have finished the work which You have given Me to do" (John 17:4 NKJV).

—*Be Resolute*, page 27

9. How did God use Daniel's health to witness to the king? What does this story teach us about the unique ways in which believers can witness to others? What are some stories from your church experience that point to the creative ways God uses people's stories to speak to nonbelievers?

Daniel did not defile himself eating food that the King asked of him - Daniel looked healthier and the King was pleased.

Deacon's Fund - Katrina - Food closet - Craft Fair - Quiet example -

From the Commentary

Each believer is either a conformer or a transformer. We're either being squeezed into the world's mold or we're transforming things in the world into which God has put us. Transformers don't always have an easy life, but it's an exciting one, and it gives us great delight to know that God is using us to influence others.

—*Be Resolute*, page 28

10. What are some of the trials Daniel endures in Daniel 1? What specific clues does he give to suggest he is not a conformer?

Not eating King's food. He convinienced the steward to let him eat vegetables. It was risky for the steward–

Daniel was taught letters and languages of the Chaldeans (this is Aramaic). Daniel would have to serve in the King's place.

Name was changed

He was loyal to the King.

Looking Inward

Take a moment to reflect on all that you've explored thus far in this study of Daniel 1. Review your notes and answers and think about how each of these things matters in your life today.

Tips for Small Groups: To get the most out of this section, form pairs or trios and have group members take turns answering these questions. Be honest and as open as you can in this discussion, but most of all, be encouraging and supportive of others. Be sensitive to those who are going through particularly difficult times and don't press for people to speak if they're uncomfortable doing so.

11. If you were in Daniel's shoes, do you think you'd be quick to deny the king's decree? Why or why not? What fears would you have to overcome to make that decision?

I would not want to go against my religious convictions– Decide I would accept the outcome if my life was put in danger.

12. Daniel took a diplomatic approach to denying the king's request (vv. 11–14). Do you tend to respond to things you don't agree with out of anger? Frustration? Or do you act more diplomatically? What is the value of Daniel's approach?

I think I am respectful to others I don't agree with. Daniel's approach is positive — He did not alienate himself.

13. In what ways do you find Daniel's decision to avoid conforming inspirational? In what ways do you find it difficult to read? What are some areas of conforming to the world that you find it hard to refuse? Why is that?

He knew God was sovereign. He had confidence God was there for him —
I don't think I want to conform to the world —

Going Forward

14. Think of one or two things that you have learned that you'd like to work on in the coming week. Remember that this is all about quality, not quantity. It's better to work on one specific area of life and do it well than to work on many and do poorly (or to be so overwhelmed that you simply don't try).

Praying and trusting God to bring a revival in our country — because it is in moral decay

Do you need to rethink those areas of your life where you tend to conform? Do you need to learn to trust God in difficult circumstances? Be specific. Go back through Daniel 1 and put a star next to the phrase or verse that is most encouraging to you. Consider memorizing this verse.

1:9 and God gave Daniel favor and compassion in the sight of the chief of the eunuch

Real-Life Application Ideas: Daniel's first trial was being asked to eat food that would have defiled him according to God's law. Take stock of the things in your life that have the potential to "defile" according to what it means to live a life pleasing to God. This could be anything from bad habits to attitudes. After making your list, spend time in prayer, asking God to give you the strength and wisdom to overcome these things.

I need to exercise for my health.

Seeking Help

15. Write a prayer below (or simply pray one in silence), inviting God to work on your mind and heart in those areas you've previously noted. Be honest about your desires and fears.

Notes for Small Groups:

- *Look for ways to put into practice the things you wrote in the Going Forward section in this lesson. Talk with other group members about your ideas and commit to being accountable to one another.*

- *During the coming week, ask the Holy Spirit to continue to reveal truth to you from what you've read and studied.*

- *Before you start the next lesson, read Daniel 2. For more in-depth lesson preparation, read chapter 2, "The God of Dreams and Destinies," in* Be Resolute.

Destiny
(DANIEL 2)

Before you begin …
- *Pray for the Holy Spirit to reveal truth and wisdom as you go through this lesson.*
- *Read Daniel 2. This lesson references chapter 2 in* Be Resolute. *It will be helpful for you to have your Bible and a copy of the commentary available as you work through this lesson.*

Getting Started

From the Commentary

As you turn from chapter 1 to chapter 2, the atmosphere in the king's palace changes radically. Chapter 1 closes with recognition and security, but chapter 2 introduces rejection and danger. Because they possessed almost unlimited power and authority, Oriental despots were notoriously temperamental and unpredictable, and here Nebuchadnezzar reveals this side of his character. (See also 3:19.) However, the hero and major actor in chapter 2 is not

King Nebuchadnezzar but the Lord God who "reveals deep and secret things" (v. 22 NKJV).

—*Be Resolute,* page 31

1. Why is there such a sudden shift in tone from chapter 1 to chapter 2? What does this say about the path Daniel's life is about to take? How does the inconsistency of the king help to underline the consistency of God's role in Daniel's life?

King Nebuchadnezzar is troubled over the dream he had and becomes desperate. Daniel relies on God and the King realizes Daniel's God is a great God.

More to Consider: Bible scholars disagree about Nebuchadnezzar's dream. Some believe the king actually forgot his dream (see vv. 5, 8). Others believe he was merely testing his advisers and that these verses reference not the dream but the king's edict of judgment. Why is this an important discussion? What are the implications of these arguments where it concerns Daniel?

2. Choose one verse or phrase from Daniel 2 that stands out to you. This could be something you're intrigued by, something that makes you uncomfortable, something that puzzles you, something that resonates with you, or

just something you want to examine further. Write that here. What strikes you about this verse?

Verse 27 - 28

There is a God in Heaven who reveals secrets

Going Deeper

From the Commentary

> Regardless of which approach is correct, this much is true: The counselors were greatly humiliated because they couldn't tell Nebuchadnezzar the dream. This was a great opportunity for them to receive wealth, prestige, and promotion, and the fact that they stalled for time indicated that they were unable to meet the challenge. This in itself set the stage for Daniel to exalt the true and living God of Israel who alone can predict the future (Isa. 41:21–23).
>
> —*Be Resolute*, page 34

3. How did the astrologers try to "buy time" in this story? (See Dan. 2:4–9.) Why do you think the king didn't want to give away the contents of the dream? How does God use the king's impossible request to set the stage for Daniel's triumph and God's own glorification?

They told the king to tell them the dream - The king thought he might me tricked and have calamity -

*More to Consider: There are lots of places in the Bible where God
exposes the foolishness of the world and the deceptiveness of Satan.
Look up some of these examples and compare them to the way God
exposes the counselors of Babylon: Moses and Aaron defeat the magicians of Pharaoh (Ex. 7—12); Elijah exposes the deception of Baal
worship (1 Kings 18); Jeremiah confronts the false prophet Hananiah (Jer. 28); Paul exposes the deception of Bar-Jesus the sorcerer
(Acts 13:1–12).*

From the Commentary

> When Arioch came to get Daniel and his friends, they were
> shocked to hear about the king's edict. As new "graduates"
> among the royal counselors, they hadn't been invited to
> the special session about the dream. Daniel spoke to Ari-
> och "with wisdom and tact" (NIV), just as he had spoken
> to Ashpenaz and Melzar (1:9–14; see Col. 4:5–6), and the
> chief executioner explained how serious the matter was.
> By doing this and delaying his obedience, Arioch was risk-
> ing his own life, but the officers in the palace had learned
> that the four Jewish men were trustworthy. Their gracious
> actions and words during their three years of training were
> now helping to save their lives.
>
> Arioch allowed Daniel time to speak to Nebuchadnezzar,
> and the king must have been surprised to see him.
>
> —*Be Resolute*, pages 35–36

4. Read Daniel 2:17–23. When Daniel returned to his friends, he urged them to plead for mercy about the mystery of the king's dream. What does this tell you about Daniel's faith? About the way he approaches challenges? What does it say to us today about how we ought to respond to difficult circumstances?

Daniel's faith was solid. He seeks God in all things

From the History Books

King Nebuchadnezzar was known not only for his military prowess but also for his leadership in building up the city of Babylon (and other surrounding areas, including a wall between the Tigris and the Euphrates meant to protect the country from invasions from the north). He is famous for sparing no expense in the capital city reconstruction, and for commissioning the Hanging Gardens of Babylon, one of the original Seven Wonders of the World. His influence was so great in the region that there aren't many places near Babylon that don't record something about him.

5. Many of Nebuchadnezzar's exploits were military, but some were more about beauty or art (as in the gardens). What does this tell you about the king's heart? History supports the notion that Nebuchadnezzar was well known and wielded great influence in the region. How might this have played into his unpredictability regarding the fortune-tellers and wise men

he surrounded himself with? Does Nebuchadnezzar's story add support to
the idea that power corrupts? Explain.

*He wanted to be seen as powerful
and in control = He was demanding
and would destroy what was in his
way. He was distrusting of others.
Beauty surrounding him was a
powerful influence on the people he
was ruled over —*

From the Commentary

> Throughout this book, Daniel and his friends are pre-
> sented as men of faith and prayer (Dan. 6; 9). They were
> far from home, but by faith they could "look toward" Jeru-
> salem and the temple and claim the promise of 1 Kings
> 8:44–45. The God of heaven would hear their prayers and
> answer them for His own glory.
>
> —*Be Resolute*, page 36

6. Read 1 Kings 8:44–45. How did Daniel and his friends claim this promise? How is this truth significant in today's culture? What are the evidences
in chapter 2 of Daniel's faith? (Circle these.)

*Claimed because they were in a different
land and were honouring God still —
Today's culture is secular. We need to
seek God's help*

More to Consider: The King James Version of the Bible uses the word "secret" ("mystery" in NIV) eight times in this chapter. Circle each use of the word. Why do you think this word is used so frequently? What is this "hidden truth" that the author is referencing?

Reinforces that God is a great God.

From the Commentary

> Once again we see the wisdom and tact of Daniel as he went immediately to Arioch and told him not to destroy the "wise men" because God had revealed to him both the dream and its interpretation. Daniel never heard the Sermon on the Mount, but he knew how to treat his enemies and was willing to rescue the pagan advisers. Since Arioch was in charge of executions, he could stop the process and save the lives of all the king's counselors in the city of Babylon. Daniel gave Arioch the privilege of taking him into the presence of the king and sharing some of the credit. The statement, "I have found a man" (v. 25) isn't exactly the truth, because it was Daniel who found Arioch; but Daniel wasn't the kind of person who worried about who got the credit so long as God got the glory.
>
> —*Be Resolute*, pages 37–38

7. Daniel could have taken all the "glory" for himself with the wisdom he had about the king's dream. What makes it possible for him to give God the glory in this life-and-death situation? Why do you think he chose to show compassion to the wise men who couldn't interpret the dream (v. 24)? What does this tell us about how we ought to respond to nonbelievers whose actions might cause us harm?

This is witness the love God has for us. God did not want Daniel to be glorified.

From the Commentary

First Daniel told the king what he had seen in his dream, and then he explained its meaning. He saw a large statue of a man, "an enormous dazzling statue, awesome in appearance" (v. 31 NIV), composed of five different materials: gold, silver, bronze, iron, and clay. Suddenly a stone appeared and smashed the feet of the statue so that the image was completely shattered and became like chaff that was blown away. Then the stone became a huge mountain that filled the earth. On hearing this accurate description, the king knew that Daniel was telling the truth and that what he said could be trusted. Only the God of heaven who sent the dream could have helped His servant know and interpret the dream.

—*Be Resolute*, page 39

8. What does this dream reveal about God's role in history? About humankind? About the coming age? About Jesus?

God is sovereign and his kingdom will not be destroyed

More to Consider: Review Daniel's interpretation of the dream in 2:36–45. How might the king have responded to this interpretation had Daniel not first recounted the dream to capture the king's trust?

The King may not have believed the interpretation —

From the Commentary

> What would all of this have meant to King Nebuchadnezzar
> as he sat on his throne listening to a young Jewish lad explain
> God's mysteries? For one thing, the message of the image
> should have humbled him. It was not Nebuchadnezzar who
> conquered nations and kingdoms; it was God who enabled
> him to do it and who gave him his empire. "You, O king,
> are a king of kings," said Daniel. "For the God of heaven
> has given you a kingdom, power, strength, and glory" (Dan.
> 2:37 NKJV). Alas, the great king forgot this lesson and one
> day said, "Is not this great Babylon, that I have built for a
> royal dwelling by my mighty power and for the honor of
> my majesty?" (4:30 NKJV). God had to humble the king and
> make him live like an animal until he learned that God does
> according to His will [4:35] and alone deserves glory.
>
> —*Be Resolute*, page 42

9. Quickly review the dream in Daniel 2:26–45. How do you think the king
felt as the details were laid out before him? What do you think surprised
him more: the fact that Daniel got the dream right, or the content of the
dream? What risks was Daniel taking in sharing this dream? How did those
risks pay off for Daniel and his friends? What does this say about God's
protection for those who trust Him?

The King was surprised

From the Commentary

> Being a pagan unbeliever, Nebuchadnezzar was so over-
> whelmed by what Daniel did that he treated him as though
> he were a god! Cornelius the Roman centurion treated
> Peter that way (Acts 10:25–26), and Paul and Barnabas
> were accepted as gods by the people of Lystra (14:8–18).
> Being a devout Jew, Daniel must have abhorred all this
> adulation, but he knew it was useless to protest the com-
> mands of the king. But in paying homage to Daniel, the
> king was actually acknowledging that the God of the
> Hebrews was greater than all other gods. Nebuchadnezzar
> hadn't yet come to the place where he believed in one true
> and living God, but this was the first step.
>
> —*Be Resolute*, page 43

10. What sort of temptations do you think Daniel faced when the king
paid him such honor after his dream interpretation? How is this situation
similar to those faced by respected church leaders today? What was Daniel's
response to the adulation? Why is it significant that Daniel asked the king
to reward his friends with key roles in the Babylonian province?

*Daniel was humble because he knew God
should be honored.
Daniel went to his friends and asked
them to seek mercy from God - They all
faced death without God revealing the
meaning of the dream.*

Looking Inward

Take a moment to reflect on all that you've explored thus far in this study of Daniel 2. Review your notes and answers and think about how each of these things matters in your life today.

Tips for Small Groups: To get the most out of this section, form pairs or trios and have group members take turns answering these questions. Be honest and as open as you can in this discussion, but most of all, be encouraging and supportive of others. Be sensitive to those who are going through particularly difficult times and don't press for people to speak if they're uncomfortable doing so.

11. In what ways have you experienced the pressure the king placed on the fortune-tellers regarding his dream? How did you respond? What role (if any) did trusting God play in your resolution of that circumstance?

12. Review Daniel's praise in 2:20–23. How do these words speak to your life circumstances today? How easy is it for you to praise God when things turn out "right"? How easy is it for you to praise God when the outcome is uncertain or not what you expected?

13. If you've ever been given praise for a particularly wise thought or action, how did that make you feel? What does it look like to give the glory to God for things you apparently do for others? How can you remain humble when God uses you to do great things? What are the challenges to this?

Going Forward

14. Think of one or two things that you have learned that you'd like to work on in the coming week. Remember that this is all about quality, not quantity. It's better to work on one specific area of life and do it well than to work on many and do poorly (or to be so overwhelmed that you simply don't try).

Do you need to be more trusting of God when things look grim? Do you need to learn humility for good things God has granted you to accomplish? Be specific. Go back through Daniel 2 and put a star next to the phrase or verse that is most encouraging to you. Consider memorizing this verse.

Real-Life Application Ideas: Consider the things in your life today that require a great deal of trust—anything from a relationship challenge to an uncertain job situation. What are you doing today to seek God's wisdom for these situations? Spend time studying Daniel's story and looking for clues about how he sought God's guidance to deal with the king's request. Then apply the same sort of wisdom to your own story.

Seeking Help

15. Write a prayer below (or simply pray one in silence), inviting God to work on your mind and heart in those areas you've previously noted. Be honest about your desires and fears.

Notes for Small Groups:

- *Look for ways to put into practice the things you wrote in the Going Forward section in this lesson. Talk with other group members about your ideas and commit to being accountable to one another.*

- *During the coming week, ask the Holy Spirit to continue to reveal truth to you from what you've read and studied.*

- *Before you start the next lesson, read Daniel 3. For more in-depth lesson preparation, read chapter 3, "Faith and the Fiery Trial," in* Be Resolute.

Faith and Fire
(DANIEL 3)

Before you begin ...
- *Pray for the Holy Spirit to reveal truth and wisdom as you go through this lesson.*
- *Read Daniel 3. This lesson references chapter 3 in* Be Resolute. *It will be helpful for you to have your Bible and a copy of the commentary available as you work through this lesson.*

Getting Started

From the Commentary

We don't know how much time elapsed between the night Nebuchadnezzar dreamed about the metallic image (Dan. 2) and the day he commanded the people to fall down before the golden image that he had made. Some students believe that the event described in Daniel 3 might have occurred twenty years after the promotion of Daniel and his friends, about the time Jerusalem was finally destroyed (586 BC)....

There was definitely an element of pride in this whole enterprise. Daniel had made it clear that no empire would last, including that of the great Nebuchadnezzar. The king's heart was filled with pride because of all his conquests, but along with that pride were fear and concern for himself and his vast kingdom. He wanted to make sure that his people were loyal to him and that there would be no rebellions.

—*Be Resolute,* pages 47–48

1. What does the king's response to Daniel's dream interpretation tell you about him? Why is it so difficult to let go of pride? How does his story mirror those of public figures in today's world?

He does not want to let go of his power—He is not trusting of anyone. No different with present day public figures—

More to Consider: It's interesting to note that there wasn't enough gold in Nebuchadnezzar's kingdom to build a solid image ninety feet high and nine feet wide, so it probably was made of wood and overlaid with gold. But it's still an impressive statue. How do you think the Babylonians would have reacted to seeing this giant statue? How might the Jews have responded? Why do you think the king chose to put this statue out on the plain?

2. Choose one verse or phrase from Daniel 3 that stands out to you. This could be something you're intrigued by, something that makes you uncomfortable, something that puzzles you, something that resonates with you, or just something you want to examine further. Write that here. What strikes you about this verse?

Verse 17 — Faithfulness to their God

Going Deeper

From the Commentary

> The king sent official messengers to all the provinces of his empire, commanding the officials to gather for the dedication of the great golden image....
>
> But this was more than a political assembly; it was a religious service, complete with music, and it called for total commitment on the part of the worshippers. Note that the word *worship* is used at least eleven times in the chapter.
>
> —*Be Resolute*, pages 48–49

3. Underline every use of the word *worship* in Daniel 3. Why is this word used so often? What does the king's command to "worship" the idol say about his arrogance? His fears? How does this sort of worship compare to that which Daniel offers to God?

Worship is forced by king — Daniel offers to God worship that is given freely of honor and love —

From the Commentary

The herald didn't ask for a vote. He simply told the people that what was about to happen was a matter of life or death. At the sound of the music, they would either fall down before the image or they would die. But the superstitious crowd was accustomed to worshipping many gods and goddesses, so the command was an easy one to obey, especially in light of the consequences.

—*Be Resolute*, page 49

4. In a culture that was accustomed to bowing before idols, the king's demand must have seemed like just another day. Why were Shadrach, Meshach, and Abednego able to disregard the king's command? Why do you suppose all of the Jews in Babylon didn't challenge the command? What are some parallels to this situation in today's culture?

Trusting their God to protect them —

From Today's World

A common theme in our culture today is that of "tolerance." This idea is often incorporated into education and the workplace and has the good intention of providing a safe environment for people with all sorts of different beliefs or lifestyles. Certainly the idea has roots in biblical truth (1 John 4:7; 1 Peter 2:17), but some Christians see the concept as being taken to an extreme that is far from biblical.

5. In what ways can "tolerance" become an idol? What is the difference between tolerance and promotion of a belief or lifestyle? What are some of the greater challenges believers face today in standing up for what they believe in?

It can become sinful and we can fall away from our faith. Believers can be persecuted—

From the Commentary

> But there were three men in that great crowd who stood tall when everybody else bowed low. Their faith was in the true and living God and in the word that He had spoken to their people. Knowing the history of the Jewish people, they were confident that the Lord was in control and they had nothing to fear.
>
> —*Be Resolute*, page 50

6. What motivated the astrologers to say to the king (about Shadrach, Meshach, and Abednego), "[They] pay no attention to you, O king" (v. 12)? How does the king's response compare to the way he dealt with things in Daniel 2? What impression do you get of him?

He is arrogant.

More to Consider: Read Isaiah 43:1–2. How do Isaiah's words speak to the circumstance these three men were facing? What does this picture of faith say about the role of feelings when it comes to obedience? Is this passage a guarantee that God will never allow us to suffer for our faith? Compare Daniel 3:17–18.

From the Commentary

[In Daniel 3:13–20,] we see the king in a fit of anger. He had conquered many cities and nations, but he could not conquer himself. "Better a patient man than a warrior, a man who controls his temper than one who takes a city" (Prov. 16:32 NIV). Yet the three Hebrew officers were calm and respectful. "Always be ready to give a defense to everyone who asks you a reason for the hope that is in you, with meekness and fear" (1 Peter 3:15 NKJV).

—*Be Resolute*, page 52

7. What were the immediate results of the king's anger (Dan. 3:19, 22)? How did God's intervention affect the king's anger? What does this tell you about the message God was sending to the king?

From the Commentary

"We are not careful to answer" (Dan. 3:16) means, "We don't need to defend ourselves or our God, for our God will defend both Himself and us." They weren't the least bit worried! It's a bit arrogant for God's people to think they have to defend God, for God is perfectly capable of defending Himself and taking care of His people. Our task is to obey God and trust Him, and He will do the rest.

—*Be Resolute*, page 53

8. What is your response to the apparent arrogance of the three men (v.16)? When do believers cross the line from appropriate confidence to inappropriate arrogance?

More to Consider: Review Hebrews 11, which lists the names and deeds of great people of faith. Hebrews 11:34 refers to these three Hebrew men who stood fast, then two verses later lists others who did not get miraculously rescued. What does this tell us about how God works His plan through the lives of His followers? How might this apply to circumstances in your church or community? Does knowing you may or may not see God's resolution of an issue give you more faith? Does it challenge your faith? Explain.

From the Commentary

The three men had refused to obey the king's order to fall down before the image, but when the king ordered them to come out of the furnace, they immediately obeyed.

—*Be Resolute*, page 55

9. Why did the three men suddenly choose to obey the king's orders after being tossed in the furnace when they didn't obey earlier (Dan. 3:26)? How can we know when it's right to challenge authority and when it's proper to obey? What guidelines should believers use in determining the proper response?

From the Commentary

> The experience of Shadrach, Meshach, and Abednego must have greatly encouraged the faithful Jews and brought conviction to the Jews who were compromising with the enemy. These three men sent a strong message to their people: Jehovah God is still on the throne, He hasn't forsaken us, and He will one day fulfill His promises to His people. He promised to be with them in their furnace of affliction if they would trust Him and obey His will. Later, when the remnant returned to the land, the account of the fiery furnace must have helped to sustain them in those years of difficulty and delay.
>
> —*Be Resolute*, page 56

10. What are some examples in today's church of believers who have encouraged others by their bold actions of faith? How are their stories like or unlike the stories of these three young men?

More to Consider: The events in Daniel 3 remind us of prophecies found in the book of Revelation (especially chapters 13 and 14). Read those chapters, then compare them to Daniel 3. How are the two passages similar? What does the book of Daniel teach us that can help us as we prepare for the end times as described in Revelation?

Looking Inward

Take a moment to reflect on all that you've explored thus far in this study of Daniel 3. Review your notes and answers and think about how each of these things matters in your life today.

Tips for Small Groups: To get the most out of this section, form pairs or trios and have group members take turns answering these questions. Be honest and as open as you can in this discussion, but most of all, be encouraging and supportive of others. Be sensitive to those who are going through particularly difficult times and don't press for people to speak if they're uncomfortable doing so.

11. When have you acted out of pride or anger as King Nebuchadnezzar did? What were the results? How might the situation have been different had you acted humbly?

12. What are some of the "idols" you bow down to? What makes it difficult for you to stand against these influences? What might Daniel say to you about standing up when the rest of the world bows down? What are some practical steps you can take to be stronger in the face of these idols?

13. In what ways are you appropriately confident about your faith? Are there ways in which you cross the line into inappropriate arrogance? Explain.

How can you live your faith confidently without being proud to the point of sinfulness?

Going Forward

14. Think of one or two things that you have learned that you'd like to work on in the coming week. Remember that this is all about quality, not quantity. It's better to work on one specific area of life and do it well than to work on many and do poorly (or to be so overwhelmed that you simply don't try).

Do you need to remove idols in your life? Do you need to become more confident about God's presence in your life? Be specific. Go back through Daniel 3 and put a star next to the phrase or verse that is most encouraging to you. Consider memorizing this verse.

Real-Life Application Ideas: Reflect on the idols you struggle with. Name them and consider what it is that draws you to bow down to them instead of trusting God. Talk with a trusted friend or pastor about how you can become stronger in your faith so you can face the idols without bowing down to them.

Seeking Help

15. Write a prayer below (or simply pray one in silence), inviting God to work on your mind and heart in those areas you've previously noted. Be honest about your desires and fears.

Notes for Small Groups:

- *Look for ways to put into practice the things you wrote in the Going Forward section in this lesson. Talk with other group members about your ideas and commit to being accountable to one another.*

- *During the coming week, ask the Holy Spirit to continue to reveal truth to you from what you've read and studied.*

- *Before you start the next lesson, read Daniel 4. For more in-depth lesson preparation, read chapter 4, "Learning the Hard Way," in* Be Resolute.

Hard Lessons
(DANIEL 4)

Before you begin …
- *Pray for the Holy Spirit to reveal truth and wisdom as you go through this lesson.*
- *Read Daniel 4. This lesson references chapter 4 in* Be Resolute. *It will be helpful for you to have your Bible and a copy of the commentary available as you work through this lesson.*

Getting Started
From the Commentary

Some students believe that twenty or thirty years may have elapsed between the episode of the fiery furnace described in chapter 3 and the events described in this chapter. Nebuchadnezzar was now enjoying a time of peace and security. After defeating all his enemies and completing several impressive building projects, he was able at last to rest at home and delight in what had been accomplished. Nebuchadnezzar thought that he was the builder of "Babylon the great" and the architect of its peace and prosperity, but he was soon to learn that all these things had been permitted by the will of the Most High God.

—*Be Resolute,* pages 61–62

1. Why do you think Daniel opens this chapter with a first-person account from Nebuchadnezzar? What tone does this set for the chapter? What attitude does the king present to the people? What thoughts does he seem to have about the God of the Israelites?

The King still thinks he controls and he does not need to answer to any one as the Most High God - He knows Daniel's God is the God to answer to but does not do it -

More to Consider: Daniel 4 is a unique chapter in the Bible because it's an official autobiographical document, prepared by the king of Babylon and distributed throughout his vast kingdom. Why was this document included? Why do you think the king was willing to openly admit his pride in this document?

2. Choose one verse or phrase from Daniel 4 that stands out to you. This could be something you're intrigued by, something that makes you uncomfortable, something that puzzles you, something that resonates with you, or

just something you want to examine further. Write that here. What strikes you about this verse?

verse 35

Going Deeper

From the Commentary

> After the first dream—that of the great image—King Nebuchadnezzar was troubled (2:3), but after this second dream, he was terrified (4:5 NIV). He summoned his wise men and asked them for the interpretation of the dream, but they were baffled; so he called for Daniel. After the experience of the first dream, when the wise men failed so miserably, you would think Nebuchadnezzar would have bypassed his advisers and called Daniel immediately. But it seems that in the record of both of these dreams, Daniel is kept apart from the wise men, even though he was "master of the magicians" (v. 9).
>
> —*Be Resolute*, page 62

3. Why do you think Daniel was kept apart from the rest of the wise men? What does it mean that Daniel was regarded as the "master of the

magicians" (v. 9 KJV)? How might God have been better glorified by Daniel being "set apart" from the rest of the wise men?

The king knew Daniel had trust in the Most High God.
Daniel wanted the King to realize and praise God.

From the Commentary

> After hearing the description of the dream, Daniel was stunned and troubled, and the king could see the perplexity on his face. Daniel's thoughts were troubled because he saw what lay ahead of the successful monarch.
>
> —*Be Resolute*, page 63

4. If Daniel had already interpreted a dream successfully for the king, why do you think he was so scared to share this interpretation? How did he go about preparing the king for the bad news?

Daniel knew to present this news in a concerned tone for the king. This should happen to your enemies not you. God saw the King's behavior and he needed to change it—

In Today's World

The delivery of bad news is never an easy thing, but technology has afforded our culture new ways to communicate such things as the end of a relationship, the end of a job, the death of a friend or relative, and so on. There are filters to "soften the blow" when people choose to relay information through phone messages or text messages or e-mail. Face-to-face conversations, like the one Daniel must have had with the king, are becoming rarer all the time in our society.

5. In Daniel's story, the king provided an opening for Daniel to soften the bad news when he said, "Do not let the dream or its meaning alarm you" (v. 19). How is this sort of give-and-take important in communication? What gets lost when information is passed along through more impersonal means? What sort of relational wisdom can we glean from Daniel's carefully worded response?

There can be a silver lining in bad news—
Bad news should be handled caringly
Caringly especially by believer of
Christ.

From the Commentary

> The grand lesson God wanted the king to learn—and that
> we must learn today—is that God alone is sovereign and
> will not permit mortals to usurp His throne or take credit
> for His works.
>
> —*Be Resolute*, page 64

6. How does Daniel present the theme of God's sovereignty in chapter 4? Underline phrases or words that point to this. What are evidences of God's sovereignty in your church community? Why is it important to be reminded of God's sovereignty?

God is in control of the kingdomes of men and he gives power to those he chooses to do so —

From the Commentary

Daniel was calling for repentance. He wanted the king to change his mind, acknowledge his sins, turn from them, and put his faith in the true and living God, the Most High God of the Hebrews. Nebuchadnezzar knew enough about Daniel's God to know that what Daniel spoke was the truth, but he did nothing about it.

—*Be Resolute*, page 66

7. What does the king's stubborn reluctance to repent say about his heart? Why, even after seeing the truth of God's power, would he continue to be so stubborn? How is this similar to the way believers today sometimes respond to God's call for repentance or heart change?

He could not move away from his view of himself as being so powerful

From the Commentary

> Nebuchadnezzar was probably walking on the flat roof of his palace, looking out over the great city when he spoke those fateful words recorded in Daniel 4:30. One thing is sure: He was walking in pride (v. 37), and pride is one of the sins that God hates (Prov. 6:16ff.).
>
> —*Be Resolute*, page 67

8. Read Daniel 4:30. What are your reactions to the king's bold proclamation? Why do you think he didn't see the error of his arrogance? How is this similar to what happens in today's world?

He looked over his city – I think he saw it as what he had accomplished –

More to Consider: God is long-suffering with sinners, but when the time comes for Him to act, there is no delay. How is this played out in Nebuchadnezzar's story? What are other stories in Scripture that point to God's long-suffering nature?

From the Commentary

> The first-person narrative picks up again in verse 34, for at
> the end of the seven years, as God had promised, Nebu-
> chadnezzar was delivered from his affliction and restored
> to sanity and normal human life. It began with the king
> lifting his eyes to God, which suggests both faith and
> submission.
>
> —*Be Resolute*, pages 68–69

9. Based on what you read in 4:34–37, do you think Nebuchadnezzar had a
spiritual conversion? What are the clues to support your answer? If so, what
was Daniel's role in preparing the way for that conversion? What does that
say about the roles we, as Christians, may play in the lives of nonbelievers
we work with and for?

He did have a spiritual conversion —
Daniel did ask the king to listen
to him and stop sinning, and God may
spare you —

From the Commentary

> What was the result of this "conversion" experience? God
> not only restored the king's reason and removed the beastly
> heart and mind, but He also graciously restored the king's

honor and splendor and gave him back his throne! He testified that he "became even greater than before" (Dan. 4:36 NIV). Where sin had abounded, grace abounded even more (Rom. 5:20).

—*Be Resolute*, page 71

10. Read Romans 5:20. How does this passage apply to the king's story? How is this conversion story similar to other stories you've read or known?

The more we see our sinfulness — the more we realize God's grace to us —

More to Consider: Read Daniel 4:37 again. Why does the king offer this warning? How does it apply to Christians today?

Looking Inward

Take a moment to reflect on all that you've explored thus far in this study of Daniel 4. Review your notes and answers and think about how each of these things matters in your life today.

Tips for Small Groups: To get the most out of this section, form pairs or trios and have group members take turns answering these questions. Be honest and as open as you can in this discussion, but most of all, be encouraging and supportive of others. Be sensitive to those who are going through particularly difficult times and don't press for people to speak if they're uncomfortable doing so.

11. This chapter of Daniel opens with a grand proclamation by the king, who later rejects God's demand for his repentance. Have you ever been quick to celebrate God's greatness one minute and disregard Him soon after? If so, what happened? Why is it so easy to go from praising God to denying Him?

12. God's response to the king's disobedience is swift. In what ways have you experienced God's swift justice? In what ways have you experienced His patience about your questionable choices or actions?

13. How does the king's apparent conversion compare with your own faith story? What truths can you see in his story (and others' conversion stories) that help shed light on your own?

Going Forward

14. Think of one or two things that you have learned that you'd like to work on in the coming week. Remember that this is all about quality, not quantity. It's better to work on one specific area of life and do it well than to work on many and do poorly (or to be so overwhelmed that you simply don't try).

Do you need to trust God's answers to difficult questions? Do you need to acknowledge God's sovereignty and be less arrogant or demanding? Be specific. Go back through Daniel 4 and put a star next to the phrase or verse that is most encouraging to you. Consider memorizing this verse.

Real-Life Application Ideas: Think about the things in your life that have humbled you most. How did pride play into those stories? Take a moment to look closely at your current life circumstances. Are there any areas where pride tends to take over? Take the next week to pray daily for God to humble you in those areas where you tend to be prideful. Invite the wise counsel of friends to weigh in on this area of your life as you attempt to hear God speak to you.

Seeking Help

15. Write a prayer below (or simply pray one in silence), inviting God to work on your mind and heart in those areas you've previously noted. Be honest about your desires and fears.

Notes for Small Groups:

- *Look for ways to put into practice the things you wrote in the Going Forward section in this lesson. Talk with other group members about your ideas and commit to being accountable to one another.*

- *During the coming week, ask the Holy Spirit to continue to reveal truth to you from what you've read and studied.*

- *Before you start the next lesson, read Daniel 5. For more in-depth lesson preparation, read chapter 5, "Numbered, Weighed, and Rejected," in* Be Resolute.

Handwriting on the Wall
(DANIEL 5)

Before you begin …
- *Pray for the Holy Spirit to reveal truth and wisdom as you go through this lesson.*
- *Read Daniel 5. This lesson references chapter 5 in* Be Resolute. *It will be helpful for you to have your Bible and a copy of the commentary available as you work through this lesson.*

Getting Started

From the Commentary

Many people who know little or nothing about the Babylonians, Belshazzar's feast, or Daniel's prophesies use the phrase "the handwriting on the wall." The phrase comes from this chapter (v. 5) and announces impending judgment.

—*Be Resolute,* page 75

1. What is the judgment announced in this chapter? Why was Daniel commended for his interpretation of the judgment, even though it was not a very pleasant outcome for the king?

King's days numbered. He would die

More to Consider: Daniel 5:1–5 gives evidence of the pride and decadence that ruled the day during Belshazzar's rule. In many ways this feast was a microcosm of the world system. How is it similar to today's world system? In what ways do people today indulge, ignorant or uncaring about any "enemy" that might be awaiting outside their gates?

2. Choose one verse or phrase from Daniel 5 that stands out to you. This could be something you're intrigued by, something that makes you uncomfortable, something that puzzles you, something that resonates with you, or just something you want to examine further. Write that here. What strikes you about this verse?

Going Deeper

From the Commentary

> Was the king drunk when he ordered the servants to bring
> in the consecrated vessels that had been taken from the
> temple in Jerusalem? [See Dan. 1:2; 2 Chron. 36:9–10.] His
> grandfather Nebuchadnezzar had decreed that all peoples
> were to give respect to the God of the Jews (Dan. 3:29),
> and he himself had praised the Lord for His sovereignty
> and greatness (4:34–37). But as the years passed, the great
> king's words were forgotten, and his grandson Belshazzar
> treated the God of Israel with arrogant disrespect.
>
> —*Be Resolute*, page 77

3. What might have caused King Nebuchadnezzar's words to be so easily forgotten? What causes people today to disregard God despite the testimony of earlier generations? What can we do to protect ourselves from becoming indifferent to God?

Prosperity. People are so blessed they forget God was the one who blessed them.

From the Commentary

> Without warning, the fingers of a human hand appeared
> in an area of the plastered wall that was illuminated by
> a lampstand, and it must have been an awesome sight.
> The revelry gradually ceased, and the banquet hall became
> deathly quiet as the king and his guests stared in amaze-
> ment at words being written on the wall.
>
> —*Be Resolute*, page 78

4. What were the words written on the wall (5:5–9)? What was significant about the timing of this message for the king? Why do you think God used such a dramatic method for delivering His message to the king?

Mene = numbered (the days of your reign)

Tekel = weighed (you have been weighed in God's balances and failed)

Parsin = divided (your kingdom will be divided and given to the Medes and Persians)

Belshazzar did not believe harm could come to him

From the History Books

It's interesting to note that while Belshazzar was enjoying his feast, the Persian army was on his doorstep, preparing to conquer Babylon. Belshazzar's father, Nabonidus, had left his son in charge of the city while he went away to devote himself to worshipping the moon god. But Nabonidus had recently returned and was defending the city to the north when the "writing on the wall" accurately predicted the imminent Persian overthrow of the city. (Nabonidus quickly surrendered and fled, paving the way for the Persian infiltration.)

5. Did Belshazzar miss obvious signs that his empire was about to fall? Did he even care? What does his feast tell you about Belshazzar's regard for the Persian army? How can power give people the impression that they're impervious to harm?

Yes – he did not believe the Persian army could conquer conquer Babylon –

From the Commentary

> Neither his exalted position nor his arrogant self-confidence could keep Belshazzar's face from turning pale, his heart from being overcome by terror, and his knees from knocking together. It must have been humiliating for the great ruler to be so out of control before so many important people.
>
> —*Be Resolute*, pages 78–79

6. How important is "image" to people in power? What role did the queen play in attempting to deal with the odd circumstances (Dan. 5:10–12)? Why do you think the king felt it necessary to promise riches to whomever could interpret the writing? *She told the king to calm himself – She knew of a man who could interpret the handwriting –*

From the Commentary

> History repeats itself (2:10–13; 4:4–7) as the counselors
> confessed their inability to interpret the message on the
> wall. Even if they could have read the words, they didn't
> have the key to deciphering the meaning of the message.
> *Mene* could mean "mina," which was a measure of money,
> or the word *numbered*. *Tekel* could mean "shekel" (another
> unit of money) or the word *weighed*; and *peres* (the plural
> is parsin) could mean "half-shekel," "half-mina," or the
> word *divided*. It could also refer to Persia!
>
> —*Be Resolute*, page 79

7. Why did the counselors confess their inability to interpret the message?
Why didn't they falsify an interpretation or tell the king it meant nothing
at all? How did God use their fears and their limited abilities to show He
was sovereign?

From the Commentary

> To the king's shame, he knew Daniel only by name and
> reputation but did not know him personally. Yet Daniel
> had "done the king's business" in the third year of his
> reign (8:1, 27), which would have been 554 BC. What a
> tragedy that the ruler of the mighty city of Babylon should
> ignore one of the greatest men in history and turn to him
> only in the last hours of his life when it was too late.
>
> —*Be Resolute*, page 81

8. Why did the king not choose to know Daniel personally? What might
have kept him from considering Daniel as a wise friend? What does this
say about Nabonidus, Belshazzar's father? What message is there in this for
us today?

From the Commentary

> Anyone who knew Aramaic could have read the words
> written on the wall, but Daniel was able to interpret their
> meaning and apply God's revelation to the people in the

banquet hall, especially the king. Daniel didn't interpret the words to signify units of money (mina, shekel, half-mina, or half-shekel) but to convey warning to the king. The word *mina* meant "numbered," and the repetition of the word indicated that God had determined and established the end of the kingdom and it would happen shortly (Gen. 41:32). Babylon's days were numbered!

—*Be Resolute*, page 83

9. The phrase "Your days are numbered" is used often in modern literature, yet it has its roots in this story. In what ways is Belshazzar's story a cautionary tale for leaders today? For people in all walks of life? What is the ultimate message of this chapter in Daniel?

From the Commentary

The phrase "that very night" (v. 30 NIV) has an ominous ring to it. "He who is often rebuked, and hardens his neck, will suddenly be destroyed, and that without remedy" (Prov. 29:1 NKJV). Belshazzar was slain that very night and the head of gold was replaced by the arms

and chest of silver. According to historians, the date was
October 12, 539 BC.

—Be Resolute, pages 83–84

10. How does this story mirror other stories where God acted immediately
to fulfill a prophecy or dream? Why does God act immediately in some
circumstances and apparently slowly in others? What does this tell us about
God's character? About His ways and means to accomplish His goals?

He is a patient God

*More to Consider: Because of high walls, guard towers, and strong
bronze gates, the people in Babylon thought they were safe from the
enemy, but the Medo-Persian army found a way to get into the city.
Isaiah had predicted the conquest of Babylon (Isa. 13—14; 21; 47).
How does the people's pride play right into this prediction? How is this
like the way pride can catch us off guard today?*

Looking Inward

Take a moment to reflect on all that you've explored thus far in this study of Daniel 5. Review your notes and answers and think about how each of these things matters in your life today.

Tips for Small Groups: To get the most out of this section, form pairs or trios and have group members take turns answering these questions. Be honest and as open as you can in this discussion, but most of all, be encouraging and supportive of others. Be sensitive to those who are going through particularly difficult times and don't press for people to speak if they're uncomfortable doing so.

11. What might your response have been if you'd seen the hand writing on the wall? Where would you have turned for answers or comfort? How is this like or unlike the way you respond to unexplainable or unexpected things in your life today?

12. Which is a greater temptation for you: taking your security for granted (and forgetting about God for stretches of time) or worrying about your security (rather than trusting God)? What would be a good attitude for you

to have about God and the risks life poses? How would that affect your actions?

13. What are areas in your life where you see "the writing on the wall"? What are the clear messages God is giving to you regarding your attitudes or behaviors? In what ways do you need to look to others for help in seeing the things God is saying to you?

Going Forward

14. Think of one or two things that you have learned that you'd like to work on in the coming week. Remember that this is all about quality, not quantity. It's better to work on one specific area of life and do it well than to work on many and do poorly (or to be so overwhelmed that you simply don't try).

Do you need to be more engaged with God regarding the battles around you? Do you need help interpreting what God might be saying to you? Be specific. Go back through Daniel 5 and put a star next to the phrase or verse that is most encouraging to you. Consider memorizing this verse.

Real-Life Application Ideas: In Belshazzar's story, the writing on the wall told him something that was too late to avoid. He was killed that night. Jesus' death and resurrection tells us that it's never too late to amend our ways. Spend a few moments this week thanking God for the second chances you've been granted by His grace. Then ask God to show you areas in your life where you can learn from His Word to avoid having to face a "writing on the wall" experience in the future.

Seeking Help

15. Write a prayer below (or simply pray one in silence), inviting God to work on your mind and heart in those areas you've previously noted. Be honest about your desires and fears.

Notes for Small Groups:

- *Look for ways to put into practice the things you wrote in the Going Forward section in this lesson. Talk with other group members about your ideas and commit to being accountable to one another.*

- *During the coming week, ask the Holy Spirit to continue to reveal truth to you from what you've read and studied.*

- *Before you start the next lesson, read Daniel 6. For more in-depth lesson preparation, read chapter 6, "Liars, Laws, and Lions," in* Be Resolute.

The Lions' Den
(DANIEL 6)

Before you begin …
- *Pray for the Holy Spirit to reveal truth and wisdom as you go through this lesson.*
- *Read Daniel 6. This lesson references chapter 6 in* Be Resolute. *It will be helpful for you to have your Bible and a copy of the commentary available as you work through this lesson.*

Getting Started

From the Commentary

As is often the case after a conquest, the new ruler wants to reorganize the government of the conquered kingdom so as to establish his authority and make things conform to his own leadership goals. But when Darius began to reorganize Babylon, he brought to light a conflict between his officers and Daniel, a veteran administrator who was now in his eighties. Today, wherever you find dedicated believers living and working with unbelievers, you will often see the same forces at work that are described in this chapter, whether in families, churches, corporations, or governments.

—*Be Resolute,* page 89

1. How are the political maneuverings in Daniel 6 similar to what goes on in businesses today? In churches? Why is it so important to the administrators that Daniel not be given a place of high standing?

Fear they will lose power, promotion wealth - Jelousey jelousey

2. Choose one verse or phrase from Daniel 6 that stands out to you. This could be something you're intrigued by, something that makes you uncomfortable, something that puzzles you, something that resonates with you, or just something you want to examine further. Write that here. What strikes you about this verse?

verse 10 — Daniel did not wavier -

Going Deeper

From the Commentary

> A wise leader first gathers information, and Darius soon
> learned about Daniel and the reputation he had for hon-
> esty and wisdom, what the KJV calls "an excellent spirit"
> (Dan. 6:3). It's likely that Daniel was in semiretirement
> at this time, but the king appointed him to be one of
> three key administrators over the kingdom. These three
> men were to manage the affairs of the 120 leaders who
> ruled over the provinces and to report directly to the king.
> Daniel proved to be such a superior worker that Darius
> planned to make him his number-one administrator over
> the entire kingdom.
>
> —*Be Resolute*, page 90

3. What does Daniel 6:3–4 tell us about Daniel's character? Why would
it be important for the new king to choose people like Daniel as his right-
hand men? What wisdom can we draw from King Darius's approach to
choosing leaders?

He was faithful, honest and smart

King could trust Daniel —

From the Commentary

> It's certainly a commendable thing when people pos-
> sess character so impeccable that they can't be accused of
> doing wrong except in matters relating to their faith. The
> conniving officers could never tempt Daniel to do any-
> thing illegal, but they could attempt to make his faithful
> religious practices illegal.
>
> —*Be Resolute*, page 91

4. How is the way the administrators attempt to orchestrate Daniel's demise
like the way corporations or organizations work today? What prompts
people to craft unethical solutions to apparent problems they're facing?
How can God work even in these deceptions to further His kingdom and
bring glory to Himself?

Rootless — whatever it takes even
propaganda — desperation —
God can expose them —

*More to Consider: Wiersbe writes, "The most important part of a
believer's life is the part that only God sees." Why is that the case?
What makes Daniel such a model for integrity?*

From Today's World

Integrity plays an important role in the business world today. More often than not, men and women of good character are rewarded for their choices by way of increased job responsibilities, raises, and promotions. But in spite of the importance placed on integrity, there are still many stories about good people who were unjustly treated by others who would stop at nothing to be rid of them. This, sadly, is also sometimes true in the local church. Sometimes rumors are started to bump someone off a committee. Other times people who disagree with leadership attempt to perform a virtual coup or end up causing a church split.

5. What is usually at the heart of ruthless or unjust treatment? Why are men and women so easily tempted to step on others in order to get ahead or get their way? What can we learn from Daniel's story about how we ought to deal with people who are trying to harm us?

jealousy — Daniel let the king handle it - he did not accuse them —

From the Commentary

Had he not been a man of faith and courage, Daniel could have compromised and found excuses for not maintaining his faithful prayer life. He might have closed his windows and prayed silently three times a day until the month was

over, or he could have left the city and prayed somewhere
else.

—*Be Resolute*, page 93

6. How might Daniel's decision to continue praying (v. 10) be construed as
stubbornness? What is the difference between stubbornness and obedience
to God? How might this story have been different had Daniel closed his
windows and prayed silently? How are Daniel's actions different from those
that Jesus denounces (Matt. 6:6; Luke 18:9–14)?

He remained obedient – He concluded
I won't be silenced.

Daniel was not self righteous or
condemning of others.

From the Commentary

The men who had spied on Daniel hurried to inform
Darius that his favorite officer had disobeyed the law and
shown disrespect to the king. It's remarkable how people
can work together quickly to do evil but find it difficult to
get together to do anything good.

—*Be Resolute*, page 94

7. Why is it often hard to work together to accomplish good things? What makes it so easy to act swiftly on evil's behalf?

Too many want to be in charge or I want it only my way— critical view —

From the Commentary

> The lions' den was a large pit divided by a moveable wall that could be pulled up to allow the lions to go from one side to the other. The keeper would put food in the empty side and lift up the wall so the lions would cross over and eat. He would quickly lower the wall and clean the safe side of the pit. The animals weren't fed often or great amounts of food so that their appetites would be keen in case there was to be an execution. Living at the gnawing edge of hunger didn't make them too tame!
>
> —*Be Resolute*, pages 95–96

8. How does God use the ill intent of the administrators to show His sovereign power? What must it have been like for Daniel to endure all of these life-and-death trials? What are Daniel's first words when he is released from the den? Why does he choose these words? How does God underline the value of integrity with this story? *Daniel was protected by God. Your Majesty, live forever — God →*

More to Consider: Review the book of Esther. How is Daniel's situation similar to the one described there? Why were rulers unwilling (or unable) to change laws, once they were "signed"? How did God work around these things to accomplish His goals in Esther's story? In Daniel's?

has sent His angel to shut the lions mouths — The evil doers were thrown to the lions —

From the Commentary

Eastern monarchs had absolute power over their subjects (5:19), and no one dared to question their decisions, let alone try to change them. Darius didn't throw all 122 officers and their families into the den of lions but only those men and their families who had accused Daniel (6:11–13).

—*Be Resolute*, page 98

9. What is significant about Darius's decision to punish only those administrators who had accused Daniel? Compare this to Nebuchadnezzar's decree in 2:12–13. Why were threats used so freely by the kings in Daniel's day? How are threats still used today by leaders to keep their followers or employees in line?

Darius ruled not by being unlawful — He did not appear arrogant like Nebuchadnezzar — Don't want to lose control —

From the Commentary

> Darius did more than execute the criminals. He also issued a decree to the whole empire, commanding his subjects to show fear and reverence to the God of Daniel, the God of the Hebrew exiles (vv. 25–27).
>
> —*Be Resolute*, page 99

10. Just as Nebuchadnezzar did in Daniel 3:29, Darius immediately acknowledged the preeminence of the God of the Israelites. Why do you think these kings were so quick to give honor to a God they didn't know personally? What does this say about what it takes to capture the attention of people with great power? How does God creatively use Daniel in each of these situations to promote the character traits of humility and obedience?

Looking Inward

Take a moment to reflect on all that you've explored thus far in this study of Daniel 6. Review your notes and answers and think about how each of these things matters in your life today.

Tips for Small Groups: To get the most out of this section, form pairs or trios and have group members take turns answering these questions. Be honest and as open as you can in this discussion, but most of all, be encouraging and supportive of others. Be sensitive to those who are going through particularly difficult times and don't press for people to speak if they're uncomfortable doing so.

11. What are examples from your life where integrity didn't pay off the way you expected? How have those affected you? How do you typically deal with situations where acting with integrity will be risky or costly for you? Why?

12. Have you ever faced oppression or persecution in the workplace? Explain. What choices did you make in light of the oppression or persecution? Did you make the right choices? Why or why not? What are some practical ways to build your faith confidence so you can live with integrity even in a hostile environment?

13. When you first came to know Christ, how did your excitement spread to others around you? Has that excitement faded? If so, why? What would it take to live daily with the same sort of adulation and thanksgiving that Darius seems to show in his decree (6:26–27)?

Going Forward

14. Think of one or two things that you have learned that you'd like to work on in the coming week. Remember that this is all about quality, not quantity. It's better to work on one specific area of life and do it well than to work on many and do poorly (or to be so overwhelmed that you simply don't try).

Do you need to evaluate your integrity? Do you need to build confidence in God? Be specific. Go back through Daniel 6 and put a star next to the phrase or verse that is most encouraging to you. Consider memorizing this verse.

> *Real-Life Application Ideas: What are the "lions' den" experiences you're facing today? In what areas of your life are you being challenged to trust God more? Make a list of these areas, then note specific things you can do to trust God despite circumstances that might seem impossible or difficult. Consider spending more time in Scripture, talking about issues with trusted friends or church leaders, and taking time for focused prayer. As you consider the challenges you're currently facing, don't forget to look back with thanksgiving on those times when God protected you from the "lions" you've already faced.*

Seeking Help

15. Write a prayer below (or simply pray one in silence), inviting God to work on your mind and heart in those areas you've previously noted. Be honest about your desires and fears.

Notes for Small Groups:

- *Look for ways to put into practice the things you wrote in the Going Forward section in this lesson. Talk with other group members about your ideas and commit to being accountable to one another.*

- *During the coming week, ask the Holy Spirit to continue to reveal truth to you from what you've read and studied.*

- *Before you start the next lesson, read Daniel 7. For more in-depth lesson preparation, read chapter 7, "Thy Kingdom Come," in* Be Resolute.

Kingdoms
(DANIEL 7)

Before you begin ...
- *Pray for the Holy Spirit to reveal truth and wisdom as you go through this lesson.*
- *Read Daniel 7. This lesson references chapter 7 in* Be Resolute. *It will be helpful for you to have your Bible and a copy of the commentary available as you work through this lesson.*

Getting Started

From the Commentary

> King Nabonidus was monarch over the empire, but he made his son Belshazzar ruler over Babylon; and the first year of his reign was probably 553. This means that the events described in chapters 7 and 8 preceded those described in chapters 5 and 6, and Daniel was nearly seventy years old at the time these events occurred.
>
> —*Be Resolute,* page 105

1. Why do you suppose Daniel arranged the material in his book so that chapters 7—8 cover events prior to those in chapters 5—6? (Keep in mind, chapter numbers weren't a part of the original manuscripts—those came later. But the order of this content was likely just as we have it recorded in the Bible.)

Because chapters 5-6 are about dreams of others, they felt he was qualified to interpret. It also showed his dependence on God.

More to Consider: The restless sea is a common biblical image for the nations of the world. Read the following Scriptures and compare them to the description Daniel offers in chapter 7: Isaiah 17:12–13; 57:20; 60:5, Ezekiel 26:3; Revelation 13:1; 17:15.

2. Choose one verse or phrase from Daniel 7 that stands out to you. This could be something you're intrigued by, something that makes you uncomfortable, something that puzzles you, something that resonates with you, or just something you want to examine further. Write that here. What strikes you about this verse?

Verse 25   3½ years of terror

Going Deeper

From the Commentary

The angel told Daniel that the four beasts represented four kingdoms (7:17), the same sequence of empires that Nebuchadnezzar had seen in his dream (chap. 2). However, the king saw a great and impressive image made of valuable metals, while Daniel saw dangerous beasts that ruthlessly devoured peoples and nations. To human eyes, the nations of the world are like Nebuchadnezzar's great image, impressive and important; but from God's viewpoint, the nations are only ferocious beasts that attack and seek to devour one another.

The lion with the wings of an eagle (Dan. 7:4) … represented the empire of Babylon, which in Nebuchadnezzar's image was the head of gold (2:37–38).

The bear with three ribs in its mouth (v. 5) … symbolized the empire of the Medes and Persians who defeated Babylon (Dan. 5).

The leopard with four wings (v. 6) … represented Alexander the Great and the swift conquests of his army, resulting in the incredible expansion of the kingdom of Greece.

The "dreadful and terrible" beast (v. 7) … represented the Roman Empire, as strong and enduring as iron and as uncompromising as a beast on the rampage.

—*Be Resolute*, pages 106–7

3. Why do you think these specific beasts were used to refer to the empires described in the excerpt? What is significant about the image of beasts in contrast to metals? What does this shift in the content of the dream tell you about Belshazzar's reign, as opposed to Nebuchadnezzar's?

These animals were most descriptive of how the people would experience their fate.

From the Commentary

> Daniel saw in his vision something that wasn't revealed to Nebuchadnezzar: The last human kingdom on earth would be a frightful kingdom, unlike any of the previous kingdoms, and it would even declare war on God! This is the kingdom of Antichrist, described in Revelation 13—19, an evil kingdom that will be destroyed when Jesus Christ returns to earth.
>
> —*Be Resolute*, page 108

4. Circle the details in this dream that are different from the one in Nebuchadnezzar's dream (Dan. 2:26–45). Why do you think this new dream had such frightening images? What message for Daniel's time was the dream presenting?

More to Consider: Skim through Revelation 13—19 in search of imagery similar to what Daniel uses in chapter 7. Write down the similar themes in the two books. What significance is there to these similarities? How was the situation facing the Babylonian Empire similar to or different from the situation facing our world today? What does this suggest about the end times?

From the History Books

History supports the accuracy of Daniel's interpretation. The Babylonian Empire ruled until the Medes and Persians overtook Babylon in 539 BC. Then, in 331 BC, Alexander the Great conquered Babylon. Rome's power flourished elsewhere soon after Babylon had essentially been dismantled and the inhabitants dispersed.

5. Why is it important that history backs up Daniel's claims? What does this suggest about the rest of Daniel's prophecies? About the prophecies that haven't yet been fulfilled?

From the Commentary

> The "little horn" (Dan 7:8, 11, 24–26) … represents the
> last world ruler, the man called Antichrist. The Greek pre-
> fix *anti* can mean "against" and "instead of." The final
> world ruler will be both a counterfeit Christ and an enemy
> who is against Christ.
>
> —*Be Resolute*, page 109

6. Read Revelation 13:1–10. What picture does John paint of this ruler
called Antichrist? How is this similar to Daniel's description of the "little
horn"? What other specific details about the Antichrist can you discern
from Daniel 7?

From the Commentary

> The "saints" are mentioned in verses 18, 21–22, 25, and
> 27, and refer to the people of God living on the earth dur-
> ing the tribulation period. The apostle John makes it clear
> that there will be believing Jews and Gentiles on the earth
> during the seven years of the tribulation (Rev. 7).

Three of the texts describe the saints as victorious over their enemies (Dan. 7:18, 22, 27), while two texts inform us that the Lord permits them to be defeated before their enemies (vv. 21, 25).

—*Be Resolute*, pages 110–11

7. Review Revelation 7. How does this passage support the idea that the "saints" referenced in Daniel 7:18, 21–22, 25, and 27 are believing Jews and Gentiles? Why do some of the texts say that the saints are victorious over their enemies while others describe how the Lord permits them to be defeated?

From the Commentary

Daniel has seen the rise and fall of five kingdoms: the Babylonians, the Medes and Persians, the Greeks, the Romans, and the kingdom of Satan headed by the Antichrist. But the most important kingdom of all is the kingdom that Christ shall establish on earth to the glory of God, the kingdom that Christians long for each time they pray, "Thy kingdom come" (Matt. 6:10).

—*Be Resolute*, pages 111–12

8. In what ways has Daniel's prophecy already been fulfilled in history? What makes it apparent that there are elements of the prophecy yet to be fulfilled? How will Christians know that the prophecy is being fulfilled?

More to Consider: Daniel's vision of God's throne parallels Ezekiel 1:15–21, 26–27. Read these passages. What does the fire represent in these visions?

9. Read 2 Samuel 7:1–17. What is the covenant God made with David? How does this promise of a "kingdom forever" line up with Daniel's prophecy in 7:26–27?

From the Commentary

> In this dramatic vision, Daniel had seen the vast sweep
> of history, beginning with the Babylonian kingdom and
> closing with the thousand-year reign of Christ on earth.
> What comfort and strength it must have given to him and
> to his people in exile that the prophecies would one day
> be fulfilled and their Messiah would reign on the throne
> of David.
>
> —*Be Resolute*, page 113

10. Daniel didn't live to see the fulfillment of every prophecy he gave. How
do you think he dealt with this reality? What do his words in 7:28 tell you
about how easy it was for him to be God's mouthpiece? What does this tell
us about our response to God when we're called to do difficult things or
when the answers to our prayers don't come as hoped?

Looking Inward

Take a moment to reflect on all that you've explored thus far in this study
of Daniel 7. Review your notes and answers and think about how each of
these things matters in your life today.

Tips for Small Groups: To get the most out of this section, form pairs or trios and have group members take turns answering these questions. Be honest and as open as you can in this discussion, but most of all, be encouraging and supportive of others. Be sensitive to those who are going through particularly difficult times and don't press for people to speak if they're uncomfortable doing so.

11. What was your reaction to Belshazzar's dream and Daniel's interpretation? In what ways do you view these as prophecies about the end times? What about the end times causes you anxiety? Hope?

12. Daniel is "troubled in spirit" (v. 15) by the visions he sees. Have you ever been troubled in spirit about the future? What prompted that anxiety? How does Daniel 7 trouble you? Inspire you?

13. What is the greatest hope you see in Daniel 7? When have you most needed to trust this hope? How can you live in light of this hope? How can you share it with others?

Going Forward

14. Think of one or two things that you have learned that you'd like to work on in the coming week. Remember that this is all about quality, not quantity. It's better to work on one specific area of life and do it well than to work on many and do poorly (or to be so overwhelmed that you simply don't try).

Do you want to better understand the prophecies in Daniel? Do you want to learn how to trust God's plan for the future? Be specific. Go back through Daniel 7 and put a star next to the phrase or verse that is most encouraging to you. Consider memorizing this verse.

Real-Life Application Ideas: There are plenty of books available today (both fiction and nonfiction) that examine the end times. Many purport to offer specific details and dates about impending events referenced in Daniel and Revelation. Read some of these resources at your local library or buy one or two from your local Christian bookstore and study what others believe about the prophecies. Decide what you believe and share that with a curious friend.

Seeking Help

15. Write a prayer below (or simply pray one in silence), inviting God to work on your mind and heart in those areas you've previously noted. Be honest about your desires and fears.

Notes for Small Groups:

- *Look for ways to put into practice the things you wrote in the Going Forward section in this lesson. Talk with other group members about your ideas and commit to being accountable to one another.*

- *During the coming week, ask the Holy Spirit to continue to reveal truth to you from what you've read and studied.*

- *Before you start the next lesson, read Daniel 8. For more in-depth lesson preparation, read chapter 8, "Beasts, Angels, and the End Times," in* Be Resolute.

End Times

(DANIEL 8)

Before you begin …
- *Pray for the Holy Spirit to reveal truth and wisdom as you go through this lesson.*
- *Read Daniel 8. This lesson references chapter 8 in* Be Resolute. *It will be helpful for you to have your Bible and a copy of the commentary available as you work through this lesson.*

Getting Started

From the Commentary

From chapter 8 to the end of the book of Daniel, the text is written in Hebrew, for the major emphasis of these chapters is God's plan for the nation of Israel in the end times. From 2:4—7:28, the book is written in Aramaic because the emphasis in those chapters is on the Gentile kingdoms in history and prophecy.

—*Be Resolute,* page 117

1. In what ways is it significant that Daniel is written in two languages? What message does this have for God's people today?

Specific to both non-Jewish and Jewish.

2. Choose one verse or phrase from Daniel 8 that stands out to you. This could be something you're intrigued by, something that makes you uncomfortable, something that puzzles you, something that resonates with you, or just something you want to examine further. Write that here. What strikes you about this verse?

Verse 24

Going Deeper

From the Commentary

It's unlikely that Daniel left Babylon and traveled to Susa to receive the vision. It's more likely that God transported him to Susa just as He transported Ezekiel to Jerusalem

(Ezek. 8; 40) and the apostle John to the wilderness (Rev. 17:3) and to the high mountain (21:10). Since Daniel was about to describe the victory of the Medes and Persians over the Babylonians, God put him into the future capital of the Persian Empire.

—*Be Resolute*, page 118

3. Read Ezekiel 8:1–6, 40:1–4, and Revelation 21:10. In what ways are these experiences similar to Daniel's? Why do you think God used such dramatic methods to communicate truths in these stories? Why doesn't God use similar methods today (or does He)?

visions or dreams - showing evil & ungodlyness - emphaying His message

From the Commentary

In the earlier part of the book, Daniel was able to interpret and explain the dreams and visions of others; but here he had to ask an angel for the meaning of the ram defeating a goat and the little horn becoming a mighty kingdom. The voice that commanded Gabriel may have been the voice of the Lord.

—*Be Resolute*, page 118

4. Why do you think Daniel needed help interpreting Belshazzar's dream
(Dan. 8:15–18)? Whose voice is the "man's voice from the Ulai" (v. 16)?
Why does the angel refer to Daniel as "son of man" (v. 17)?

*God chose to handle it that way—
"Son of man" — Gabriel called
Jesus "Son of God"*

*More to Consider: Gabriel appears other times in the Bible. Look up
the following Scriptures and compare his appearance to that found in
Daniel: Luke 1:11–20; Luke 1:26–38.*

From the History Books

In the early 1800s, William Miller, an American Baptist preacher, began to
study the Bible closely in an attempt to harmonize the apparent contradic-
tions in Scripture. He eventually became convinced that the precise time of
Christ's second coming was revealed in Bible prophecy, principally in Daniel 8:14. He made some assumptions on the dates, did some calculation,
and ended up determining that Jesus would return in 1843. The saying
"1843 will be the year of jubilee" became the "theme" of his apparent discovery, and many believers got excited about the possibility that he could
be right. He even landed on a specific date, October 22. But when October 23
came and went like any other, Miller and his followers realized his calcula-
tions had been in error. Despite this "Great Disappointment," Miller's

emphasis on the "soon coming of Christ" led to the development of a number of major denominations, including the Seventh Day Adventists and the Advent Christian Church.

5. Why do you think William Miller (and others before and after him) believed he had discovered the secret to prophecies about Christ's return? Why do you think people were quick to follow him? Why didn't they all fall away after he was proven wrong? What positive results might have come from Miller's mistakes?

From the Commentary

> The imagery used in connection with Cyrus is fascinating. He is called "the righteous man" (Isa. 41:2), or as the NIV puts it, "calling him in righteousness." This means that he was called to fulfill God's righteous purposes in freeing Israel from their Babylonian yoke and allowing them to return to their land. Our sovereign Lord can use even a pagan king to accomplish His purposes!
>
> —Be Resolute, pages 119–20

6. Daniel 8:3-4, 20 alludes to the Persian conquest of much of the Middle East in the sixth century BC. King Cyrus of Persia is referenced specifically in Daniel 1:21 and 6:28 as well as in Ezra 1:1–4. Why do you think God chose to use a pagan nation led by a powerful nonbeliever to accomplish His goals? How did God use this "two-horned ram" for His purposes? What are other examples in history where God used nonbelievers to accomplish His purposes?

God knew they would do what he called them to do.
Book of Jonah

More to Consider: Despite his reputation as a powerful military leader, Cyrus was also known as a statesman who didn't attempt to dismantle religions and instead offered generosity rather than repression. How might this approach to conquest have influenced the manner in which God used him to work toward the release of the Jews from captivity?

From the Commentary

In Nebuchadnezzar's image, Greece was depicted as the thigh of brass (2:32, 39), and in Daniel's vision described in chapter 7, Greece was a swift leopard with four heads. Now Daniel sees Greece as an angry goat who runs so swiftly his feet don't even touch the ground! The large protruding horn represents Alexander the Great, who led the armies of Greece from victory to victory and extended his empire even beyond what Cyrus had done with the Persian army. But the horn was broken, for Alexander died in Babylon in June 323 [BC], at the age of thirty-three, and his vast kingdom was divided among four of his leaders, symbolized by the four horns that grew up (see 7:4–7; 11:4).

—*Be Resolute*, page 120

7. Underline the three descriptions of Alexander the Great and his Greek empire from the three dreams (chapters 2, 7, 8). What does the progression from one to the next say about Alexander's power? These images seem to support the historical record of Alexander's conquests and ultimate demise. How important is it that history back up the truths of Scripture?

More to Consider: A king named Antiochus IV inherited part of Alexander's empire. He gave himself the name "Epiphanes," which means "illustrious manifestation," for he claimed to be a revelation (epiphany) of the gods. What does this tell you about Antiochus?

From the Commentary

> What Antiochus did was a foreshadowing of what the
> Antichrist will do when he puts his image in the tem-
> ple and commands the world to worship him (2 Thess. 2;
> Rev. 13). Daniel 8:13 and 11:31 refer to Antiochus, and
> the other references to Antichrist, of whom Antiochus is
> a picture.
>
> —*Be Resolute*, page 123

8. Some scholars believe that the events described in Daniel have already
occurred, that it is not a prophecy of the end times yet to come but a
prophecy that was fulfilled in the time of Antiochus. What evidence from
Scripture might support this theory? In what ways might the prophecies be
both fulfilled and yet to be fulfilled? How is the reference to Antiochus in
8:13 an example of this?

From the Commentary

> The angel awakened Daniel from his deep sleep and told
> him there was yet more prophetic truth for him to hear,

and it related to "the time of wrath" (v. 19 NIV) and the "time of the end" (vv. 17, 19), which is the time of tribulation. The Old Testament prophets called this period "the time of Jacob's trouble" and "the day of the LORD," the period when God's wrath would be poured out on an evil world.

—*Be Resolute*, page 124

9. It seems Daniel was particularly exhausted and troubled by the visions given him in 8:19–25 (see v. 27). Why would these visions have troubled him more than any of the others he'd seen? What does this tell us about the importance of the prophecies?

More to Consider: Compare verses 23–27 with 9–14. In what ways do the characteristics of Antiochus parallel those of the Antichrist?

From the Commentary

> Daniel is a good example for students of prophecy to fol-
> low. He asked the Lord for the explanation (Dan. 8:15)
> and allowed the Lord to instruct him. But his investigation
> into God's prophetic program wasn't a matter of satisfying
> curiosity or trying to appear very knowledgeable before
> others. He was concerned about his people and the work
> they had to do on earth.
>
> —*Be Resolute*, page 125

10. In what ways are Daniel's actions as a prophet a good model for us as
students of Scripture? What can we learn from his methods that can help
us mature as believers and be better prepared to answer questions posed by
nonbelievers?

Looking Inward

Take a moment to reflect on all that you've explored thus far in this study
of Daniel 8. Review your notes and answers and think about how each of
these things matters in your life today.

Tips for Small Groups: To get the most out of this section, form pairs or trios and have group members take turns answering these questions. Be honest and as open as you can in this discussion, but most of all, be encouraging and supportive of others. Be sensitive to those who are going through particularly difficult times and don't press for people to speak if they're uncomfortable doing so.

11. What questions or fears do you have about the end times? In what ways are Daniel's visions encouraging to you? Confusing? Inspiring? How do you think we are meant to live in light of them?

12. What are some of the ways God chooses to speak to you? How would you react to prophetic visions like Daniel was given? What sort of burden did he carry for God's people? What are the burdens you carry for fellow believers and nonbelievers today?

13. What's most important for you to know about the end times? Do you place too much or not enough emphasis on these events? How do you go about studying these things?

Going Forward

14. Think of one or two things that you have learned that you'd like to work on in the coming week. Remember that this is all about quality, not quantity. It's better to work on one specific area of life and do it well than to work on many and do poorly (or to be so overwhelmed that you simply don't try).

Do you need to learn more about the end times? Do you want to discover more about the history described in Daniel's visions? Be specific. Go back through Daniel 8 and put a star next to the phrase or verse that is most encouraging to you. Consider memorizing this verse.

Real-Life Application Ideas: Research the stories of people like William Miller—people who believed they knew the time of Jesus' second coming. Consider what prompted them to pursue this line of study. Then think about your own life—in what ways are you living expectantly? What is the value of living as if Jesus will return soon? How can you apply these truths to your daily life?

Seeking Help

15. Write a prayer below (or simply pray one in silence), inviting God to work on your mind and heart in those areas you've previously noted. Be honest about your desires and fears.

Notes for Small Groups:

- *Look for ways to put into practice the things you wrote in the Going Forward section in this lesson. Talk with other group members about your ideas and commit to being accountable to one another.*

- *During the coming week, ask the Holy Spirit to continue to reveal truth to you from what you've read and studied.*

- *Before you start the next lesson, read Daniel 9—10. For more in-depth lesson preparation, read chapters 9 and 10, "The Prophetic Calendar" and "A Remarkable Experience," in* Be Resolute.

A Concerned Prophet
(DANIEL 9—10)

Before you begin …
- *Pray for the Holy Spirit to reveal truth and wisdom as you go through this lesson.*
- *Read Daniel 9—10. This lesson references chapters 9 and 10 in* Be Resolute. *It will be helpful for you to have your Bible and a copy of the commentary available as you work through this lesson.*

Getting Started

From the Commentary

The first year of Darius was 539 BC, the year that Babylon fell to the Medes and the Persians. This great victory was no surprise to Daniel, because God had already told him that the Medo-Persian Empire would conquer Babylon. In Nebuchadnezzar's great "dream image," the head of gold would be replaced by the chest and arms of silver (chap. 2); and later visions revealed that the bear would conquer the lion (chap. 7). But long before Daniel's day, both Isaiah and Jeremiah had predicted the fall of Babylon, so it's no surprise that Daniel started studying afresh the scroll of the prophet Jeremiah.

—*Be Resolute,* pages 129–30

✓ 1. What is the purpose of Daniel's prayer (9:4–19)? Why does he plead with God not to delay? What is the significance of his mentioning God's delivery of the Israelites from Egypt?

Daniel pleads for Jerusalem.
Because Jerusalem lies in ruins —
don't delay. The city bears your
name — Daniel wants Jerusalem
restored for Glory to God.
Delivering the Jews from Egypt brought
honor to God in a great display of
power —

More to Consider: Read Jeremiah 24—25. How might Daniel have responded to these words? In what ways would they reassure him? What would he have learned about the exile? The defeat of Babylon?

Daniel could have responded by asking for mercy.
Reassure him because of his dreams. Jeremiah prophe
captivity —

2. Choose one verse or phrase from Daniel 9—10 that stands out to you. This could be something you're intrigued by, something that makes you uncomfortable, something that puzzles you, something that resonates with you, or just something you want to examine further. Write that here. What strikes you about this verse?

9:4 Our God is merciful.

Going Deeper

From the Commentary

> Daniel is a wonderful example of balance in the spiritual
> life, for he devoted himself to both the Word of God and
> prayer (Acts 6:4). Some believers are so wrapped up in pro-
> phetic studies that they have little concern for the practical
> outworking of God's will. All they want to do is satisfy
> their curiosity and then proudly share their "insights" with
> others. When Daniel learned God's truth, the experience
> humbled him and moved him to worship and to pray.
>
> —*Be Resolute*, page 133

3. What are the steps Daniel took to pray for God's mercy (Daniel 9:3–19)?
What are the various elements of his prayer? How is this like and unlike the
manner in which Christians often pray today?

— Confession of sin. — fasting, sackcloth
& ashes —
— adoration

Christians pray to Jesus — covenant —
Blood of Jesus.

From the Commentary

> While Daniel's prayer was certainly personal, he so iden-
> tified with the people of Israel that his prayer involved

national concerns. The pronoun he uses is "we" rather than "they" or "I." He confessed that he and the people had sinned greatly against the Lord and broken the terms of His gracious covenant.

—*Be Resolute*, page 135

4. According to Daniel 9:5–6, what were the Israelites' sins? What were the consequences of their rebellion (v. 8)? What does Daniel ask of God in Daniel 9:16–19?

Turned away from commandments. Have not listened to the prophets servants of God.

City of Jerusalem — prayer God would turn away his anger and wrath on Jerusalem asking for Mercy.

From Today's World

In a culture where everything is essentially only a mouse-click away, patience has become something of a lost art. No longer do people have to wait in line at a store to purchase something, nor do they have to spend hours at the local library to research answers to questions. The Internet age has become an age of "shortcuts" to information, communication, and consumerism. Our world today seems in sharp contrast to that of the Israelites who endured years upon years of "waiting on God."

5. What unique value is there in learning to wait? How does our culture today make that difficult? In what ways are Christians today "waiting on

God"? What can we learn from the Israelites' patience (and impatience) to help with our own faith journeys?

From the Commentary

> While Daniel was praying, the angel Gabriel came swiftly to him, interrupted his prayer, touched him, and spoke to him. Daniel had met Gabriel after seeing the vision of the ram and the goat, and Gabriel had explained its meaning to him (Dan. 8:15ff.). Now the angel had come to explain to Daniel what God had planned for Jerusalem, the temple, and the Jewish people.
>
> —*Be Resolute*, page 138

Daniel 9:22–27

having an ambiguous or hidden meaning

6. Why are there so many cryptic references in books like Daniel? How does the manner in which God speaks to Daniel (and others throughout biblical history) help us to know God Himself?

Because God wants Daniel to seek Him. The prophecies lead to repentance. Daniel ask God to forgive the sins of the Jews. Prophecy is God's word. It is not of private interpretation.

More to Consider: The last chapters of Daniel are stuffed full of dates and years and events that require careful study to begin to understand. If you have a copy of Be Resolute *available, read chapters 9 and 10 to gain a better understanding of the significance of these dates. Why do you think these chapters are included in Daniel? What is the value of these (and other) difficult-to-understand passages in Scripture?*

From the Commentary

For three weeks, Daniel had fasted and prayed and used no ointments as he sought the face of the Lord. Why? One reason was probably his concern for the nearly fifty thousand Jews who a year before had left Babylon and traveled to their native land to rebuild the temple. Since Daniel had access to official reports, he no doubt heard that the remnant had arrived safely in Jerusalem and that all of the tabernacle treasures were intact.

—*Be Resolute,* page 146

7. Why do you think Daniel stayed behind in Babylon after the Jews had been freed to return and rebuild the temple (Dan. 10:1–2)? How might his continued presence in Babylon, under the Medo-Persian rule, have been important to the remnant of the Jewish nation?

From the Commentary

> Three days after the end of his fast, Daniel saw an awe-some vision as he stood by the Tigris River. Why Daniel was there isn't explained in the text, but it was the place where God met with him and revealed Israel's future in the greatest prophecy God ever gave to His servant.
>
> —*Be Resolute*, page 147

The angel Michael guards the people of Israel —

✔ 8. Read Daniel 10:4–9, 14. What happened to Daniel? Why was this such a significant prophecy to the Israelites? Why do you think God chose to reveal this prophecy after Daniel's fast?

Daniel prepared to receive the vision — with fasting and prayer. Strength left Daniel. —

From the Commentary

> At the beginning of Daniel's prophetic ministry, he inter-preted the meaning of the awesome image that King Nebuchadnezzar had seen in his dream (Dan. 2), and now at the end of his ministry, Daniel saw an even greater sight—the glorious King of Kings and Lord of Lords! When we know that Jesus is standing with us and fighting

for us, we can accept any circumstance and accomplish any task He gives us.

—*Be Resolute*, page 149

9. Why are there repeated encouragements to "not be afraid" in Daniel's vision? How is this similar to the message angels have given throughout Scripture? How would the vision in Daniel 10 have compared to the previous vision, which had troubled Daniel greatly?

From the Commentary

Daniel's conversation with the angel reveals to us the important fact that there is an "invisible war" going on in the heavenlies between the forces of evil and the forces of God. For three weeks, Daniel had been praying for wisdom to understand the visions he had already seen, but the answer to that prayer was delayed. Why would the Lord not immediately answer the petitions of His beloved prophet? Because "the prince of the kingdom of Persia"— an evil angel—had attacked the angel bearing the answer, probably Gabriel. This evil angel was assigned to see to it that the king of Persia did what Satan wanted him to do. Michael, the archangel assigned to minister to Israel (Dan. 12:1; Rev. 12:7; Jude 9), assisted Gabriel and together they won the battle.

Well-meaning people may scoff at the idea of demonic forces and good and evil angels, and they may caricature Satan, but the fact remains that this is biblical theology.

—*Be Resolute*, page 151

10. Circle phrases or words in Daniel 10 that suggest an "invisible war" is going on. Why is this important for Daniel to understand? Why is it important for us to understand today? How does the truth of a spiritual battle help us in everyday life?

Looking Inward

Take a moment to reflect on all that you've explored thus far in this study of Daniel 9—10. Review your notes and answers and think about how each of these things matters in your life today.

Tips for Small Groups: To get the most out of this section, form pairs or trios and have group members take turns answering these questions. Be honest and as open as you can in this discussion, but most of all, be encouraging and supportive of others. Be sensitive to those who are going through particularly difficult times and don't press for people to speak if they're uncomfortable doing so.

11. Review Daniel's prayer in 9:4–19. In what ways can you resonate with the content of this prayer? When have you turned away from God? In what aspects of your life do you long for God to act quickly?

12. God's promise to rebuild the temple is supported by the visions Daniel receives. What are some of the promises you are counting on in your relationship with God? What does God's answer to the Israelites' captivity (and the way in which it came about) tell you about how God accomplishes His purposes? How do you know when the things you're hoping for are aligned with God's purposes?

√ 13. If Jesus were to appear to you right at this moment, what would your response be? In what ways would your response be like Daniel's response to the vision of the King of Kings? What would you want to ask Him? How would you react if you were the only one to see Him?

Going Forward

14. Think of one or two things that you have learned that you'd like to work on in the coming week. Remember that this is all about quality, not quantity. It's better to work on one specific area of life and do it well than to work on many and do poorly (or to be so overwhelmed that you simply don't try).

Do you need to ask God for forgiveness? Do you need to spend time in prayer, inviting God's will to be made known to you? Be specific. Go back through Daniel 9—10 and put a star next to the phrase or verse that is most encouraging to you. Consider memorizing this verse.

> *Real-Life Application Ideas: Think about the things you've been asking God for. How has He already answered these prayers? What answers are you still awaiting? Think about the long history of the Israelites and God's unexpected answers to their prayers, then ask God to give you patience and wisdom as you wait for answers to those things most important to you.*

Seeking Help

15. Write a prayer below (or simply pray one in silence), inviting God to work on your mind and heart in those areas you've previously noted. Be honest about your desires and fears.

Notes for Small Groups:

- *Look for ways to put into practice the things you wrote in the Going Forward section in this lesson. Talk with other group members about your ideas and commit to being accountable to one another.*

- *During the coming week, ask the Holy Spirit to continue to reveal truth to you from what you've read and studied.*

- *Before you start the next lesson, read Daniel 11—12. For more in-depth lesson preparation, read chapters 11 and 12, "A Remarkable Prophecy—Part I" and "A Remarkable Prophecy—Part II," in* Be Resolute.

A Host of Prophecies

(DANIEL 11—12)

Before you begin ...

- *Pray for the Holy Spirit to reveal truth and wisdom as you go through this lesson.*
- *Read Daniel 11—12. This lesson references chapters 11 and 12 in* Be Resolute. *It will be helpful for you to have your Bible and a copy of the commentary available as you work through this lesson.*

Getting Started

From the Commentary

The prophecy given in chapters 11 and 12 is long and complex. The first thirty-five verses of Daniel 11 were prophecy in Daniel's day but are now history. They deal with important but, for the most part, forgotten historical characters with difficult names and complicated relationships. The chapters may be outlined as follows:

Prophecies already fulfilled (Daniel 11:1–35)

Prophecies yet to be fulfilled (Daniel 11:36—12:3)

Final instructions to Daniel (Daniel 12:4–13)

—*Be Resolute,* page 157

1. How do fulfilled prophecies prove the inspiration of Scripture? What does Daniel's accuracy about fulfilled prophecies tell us about the prophecies as yet unfulfilled? How does waiting on God's timing to fulfill prophecies build our faith?

These prophecies are from God—must be interpreted for by those sent from God. We have God's promise, we can trust His promise—

2. Choose one verse or phrase from Daniel 11—12 that stands out to you. This could be something you're intrigued by, something that makes you uncomfortable, something that puzzles you, something that resonates with you, or just something you want to examine further. Write that here. What strikes you about this verse?

Going Deeper

From the Commentary

> The nations here are Egypt (south) and Syria (north), and
> the rulers change regularly. The little nation of Israel was
> caught between these two great powers and was affected
> by their conflicts. All of these people and events may not
> be interesting to you, but the prophecies Daniel recorded
> tally with the record of history, thus proving that God's
> Word can be trusted.
>
> —*Be Resolute*, pages 161–62

3. In what ways is the Bible a historical record? How is this evident in Daniel?
In what ways does this add credibility to the rest of Scripture? What do you
think we are meant to learn about God and history from Daniel 11?

What was prophesided occurred—
God's word can be trusted—

From the Commentary

> According to [Daniel 11:33–35], there was a small group of
> faithful Jews who opposed the godlessness of Antiochus and
> trusted God to enable them to fight back. A Jewish priest

named Mattathias, with his five sons, gathered an army and
were able to fight back. His son Judas, nicknamed Macca-
beus ("the hammerer"), was one of the heroes of this revolt.
Many Jews laid down their lives for their city, their temple,
and their faith, and finally they won. On December 14,
165, the temple was purified and the altar dedicated. (See
8:9–14, 23–25.) The Jews celebrate this occasion annually
as the Feast of Lights (Hanukkah).

—*Be Resolute*, pages 165–66

4. These prophecies of Syria and its leader, Antiochus Epiphanes (whom we
met earlier in chapter 8), describe not only his rise to power, but also the
revolt led by Mattathias and his sons that eventually led to his defeat. It's
interesting to note that the prophecy describes how many of the faithful will
fall in battle. How might this sort of prophecy have been received by the
faithful Jews? What sort of encouragement might it have brought? What
fears might it have stirred in them?

*More to Consider: If you have access to a history book (or the Internet),
do a little research on any of the rulers described in Daniel 11:5–20.*

How does reading about these rulers in nonbiblical sources affect your reading of this passage in Scripture?

From the History Books

There are plenty of stories in church history about people who claimed to have the truth about current or future events. Even today, many so-called "modern day prophets" claim access to knowledge about the future, whether from God or other sources. (The prophet is not exclusively a Judeo-Christian idea. Prophets are also notable in Islam and have been a part of pagan cultures for centuries.) However, the test of a true prophet is rarely (if ever) met by these people—the ability to claim 100 percent accuracy with predictions.

5. Why do we not see the same sort of prophecy that the Jews did in Daniel's day? How do modern prophets differ from the prophets of old? Does God still raise up prophets? If so, how do we know they're truly from God?

Prophecies have been given—don't need them —

From the Commentary

At Daniel 11:36, the prophecy shifts from Antiochus Epiphanes to the man he foreshadowed, the Antichrist, the last world dictator. We have moved to "the time of the end" (v. 35; see 12:4), when the following events are predicted to occur:

The rise of the Antichrist (Daniel 11:36–39)

The tribulation (Daniel 12:1)

War and invasions (Daniel 11:40–43)

The battle of Armageddon (Daniel 11:44–45a)

The return of Christ to defeat Antichrist (Daniel 11:45b)

The resurrection of the dead (Daniel 12:2)

The glorious kingdom (Daniel 12:3)

—*Be Resolute*, page 169

6. What is your reaction to Wiersbe's interpretation above? What are the implications for how we proceed in faith while we anticipate these events?

From the Commentary

> Throughout the last three and a half years of the tribulation period, nations will submit to the rule of Antichrist, but there will be growing dissent and opposition, even though his work is energized by Satan.

> —*Be Resolute*, page 172

7. As Daniel describes it in Daniel 11:44–45, what is this "tribulation" period? What makes end times theology controversial? How important is it to our daily living to understand Daniel's prophecies? Why?

From the Commentary

> As the huge army from the east gets positioned to attack the forces of Antichrist in Israel, the sign of the returning Son of Man will appear in the heavens (Matt. 24:29–30), and the opposing armies will unite to fight Jesus Christ. But the Lord will descend from heaven with His armies, defeat both armies, and take captive Satan, Antichrist, and the false prophet and cast them into the lake of fire (Rev. 19:11–21;

see also Zech. 12:1–9; 14:1–3). "He [Antichrist] shall come to his end, and no one shall help him" (Dan. 11:45).

—*Be Resolute*, page 172

8. God gave this prophecy to the Jews under foreign domination more than two thousand years ago, well before the first coming of Christ. What do you think they were meant to learn from it that was relevant to the way they lived their daily lives? What do you think we are meant to learn from it that is relevant today? What impression of God and the way He works in history does Daniel 11—12 give you?

To show them how to live Godly lives – same today too –

More to Consider: The doctrine of the resurrection of the human body is hinted at in Daniel 12:2, but isn't presented with the same clarity as in the New Testament. Why do you think this is so? What are some of the other hints in the Old Testament about the doctrine?

9. Read Daniel 12:5–10. What answer did Daniel get when he asked when all of these prophecies would be fulfilled? What is the significance of that answer? Why does the "man in linen" tell Daniel to "go your way" (12:9)? Why are there specific days given to the prophecy in 12:11–12?

From the Commentary

"How long?" and "How will it end?" are questions that we ask when the times are difficult and the future in doubt. "What's the purpose of it all?" Daniel did what all of us must do: he humbly asked God for the wisdom that he needed. But He may not tell us (Deut. 29:29)! He knows how much we need to know and how much we can take (John 16:12). He did promise that all these things would be clearer for those living in the end times, which is an encouragement for us to prayerfully study the prophetic Scriptures.

But the Lord did reveal that, in the end times, as trials come to the people on the earth, these trials will make the believers purer and wiser, but the wicked will only become more wicked.

—*Be Resolute*, page 177

10. How will we know when we're in the end times as described by Daniel? What clues will we have that the events prophesied are coming true? What does this tell us about how we should live our lives today? What does it mean to be "prepared" for the end times?

Looking Inward

Take a moment to reflect on all that you've explored thus far in this study of Daniel 11—12. Review your notes and answers and think about how each of these things matters in your life today.

Tips for Small Groups: To get the most out of this section, form pairs or trios and have group members take turns answering these questions. Be honest and as open as you can in this discussion, but most of all, be encouraging and supportive of others. Be sensitive to those who are going through particularly difficult times and don't press for people to speak if they're uncomfortable doing so.

11. Have you ever encountered someone who claimed to know the future? What were the circumstances of that encounter? What did the person tell you? How was this like or unlike the way the biblical prophets spoke of forthcoming events?

12. What have you learned about the end times that has helped you to grow in faith? Have you discovered anything about the end times that has clouded your understanding? What role does an understanding of the end times play in your daily life?

13. How important is it to you to understand what's to come? What role does faith play in our exploration of the end times? How might God be using the mystery of these events to accomplish His purposes?

Going Forward

14. Think of one or two things that you have learned that you'd like to work on in the coming week. Remember that this is all about quality, not quantity. It's better to work on one specific area of life and do it well than to work on many and do poorly (or to be so overwhelmed that you simply don't try).

Do you want to study more about the tribulation? Do you need to live with more confidence in a God who has all of history under control? Be specific. Go back through Daniel 11—12 and put a star next to the phrase or verse that is most encouraging to you. Consider memorizing this verse.

Real-Life Application Ideas: There are lots of resources exploring Daniel's prophecies (and the prophecies in Revelation). Take an afternoon to visit a library or do research online to find out the different views on the second coming and how it relates to the Old and New Testament prophecies. Then talk with a friend about what you discover. Pray for understanding as you examine these materials, and particularly for wisdom on how these things matter to your daily walk of faith.

Seeking Help

15. Write a prayer below (or simply pray one in silence), inviting God to work on your mind and heart in those areas you've previously noted. Be honest about your desires and fears.

Notes for Small Groups:

- *Look for ways to put into practice the things you wrote in the Going Forward section in this lesson. Talk with other group members about your ideas and commit to being accountable to one another.*

- *During the coming week, ask the Holy Spirit to continue to reveal truth to you from what you've read and studied.*

Summary and Review

Notes for Small Groups: This session is a summary and review of this book. Because of that, it is shorter than the previous lessons. If you are using this in a small-group setting, consider combining this lesson with a time of fellowship or a shared meal.

Before you begin…
- *Pray for the Holy Spirit to reveal truth and wisdom as you go through this lesson.*
- *Briefly review the notes you made in the previous sessions. You will refer back to previous sections throughout this bonus lesson.*

Looking Back

1. Over the past twelve lessons, you've examined the book of Daniel. What expectations did you bring to this study? In what ways were those expectations met?

2. What is the most significant personal discovery you've made from this study?

3. What surprised you most about Daniel's prophecies? About Daniel's character? What, if anything, troubled you?

Progress Report

4. Take a few moments to review the Going Forward sections of the previous lessons. How would you rate your progress for each of the things you chose to work on? What adjustments, if any, do you need to make to continue on the path toward spiritual maturity?

5. In what ways have you grown closer to Christ during this study? Take a moment to celebrate those things. Then think of areas where you feel you still need to grow and note those here. Make plans to revisit this study in a few weeks to review your growing faith.

Things to Pray About

6. Daniel is packed with familiar stories and rich history. As you reflect on this book, ask God to reveal to you those truths that you most need to hear. Revisit Daniel often and seek the Holy Spirit's guidance to gain a better understanding of what it means to be resolute.

7. Daniel covers a wide variety of topics, including trusting God, the value of listening to God, future events, patience, and God's sovereignty. Spend time praying about each of these topics.

8. Whether you've been studying this in a small group or on your own, there are many other Christians working through the very same issues you discovered when examining the book of Daniel. Take time to pray for each of them, that God would reveal truth, that the Holy Spirit would guide you, and that each person might grow in spiritual maturity according to God's will.

A Blessing of Encouragement

Studying the Bible is one of the best ways to learn how to be more like Christ. Thanks for taking this step. In closing, let this blessing precede you and follow you into the next week while you continue to marinate in God's Word:

May God light your path to greater understanding as you review the truths found in Daniel and consider how they can help you grow closer to Christ.

The "BE" series . . .

For years pastors and lay leaders have embraced Warren W. Wiersbe's very accessible commentary of the Bible through the individual "BE" series. Through the work of Cook International, the "BE" series is part of a library of books made available to indigenous Christian workers. These are men and women who are called by God to grow the kingdom through their work with the local church worldwide. Here are a few of their remarks as to how Dr. Wiersbe's writings have benefited their ministry.

"Most Christian books I see are priced too high for me . . .
I received a collection that included 12 Wiersbe
commentaries a few months ago and I have
read every one of them.
I use them for my personal devotions every day and they
are incredibly helpful for preparing sermons.
The contribution Cook International is making to the
church in India is amazing."

—Pastor E. M. Abraham, Hyderabad, India